CW01594347

Apostle of God

edited by

Mohammad Ali Shomali

Islamic Reference Series:

Vol. 3 Apostle of God

Edited by Mohammad Ali Shomali

First published in Great Britain in 2009

ISBN: 1-904934-15-3

978-1-904934-15-8

Published by

Institute of Islamic Studies
Islamic Centre of England
140 Maida Vale, London W9 1QB
Tel: (44) 0207 604 5500; Fax: (44) 0207 604 4898
Email: ic-el@ic-el.com

بسم الله الرحمن الرحيم

In the Name of God,

the Most Gracious, the Most Merciful

Table of contents

Preface

After the Glorious Qur'an, the character and sayings of the Prophet Muhammad form a major source for any study of Islam. The Qur'an itself introduces the Prophet Muhammad as a perfect role model, in whom there is a good example for all the believers (33:21). The Prophet Muhammad was responsible for explaining the Qur'an (16:44), for the purification of people and for teaching them the Qur'an and wisdom (62:2). He never spoke of his own wish (53:3). Muslims are asked to hold on to whatever he gave them and refrain from whatever he prohibited (59:7).

Thus, every aspect of his character and conduct, including the noble traits of his character, words and deeds are to be followed. The papers in this volume discuss various aspects of the life, character and teachings of the Prophet Muhammad.

The first paper is entitled "A Glimpse of the Character Traits of the Prophet Muhammad." In this paper, Ayatollah Sayyid Abu'l-Fadl Mujtahid Zanjani reviews the life and conduct of the Prophet Muhammad in a scholarly manner. The paper first appeared in Persian under the title '*Gush-i'i az Akhlāq-i Muhammad*' ('A Glimpse of the Character Traits of the Prophet Muhammad') in the book '*Muhammad Khātam-i Payāmbarān*' (*Muhammad, the Seal of the Prophets*), Husayniyyah-i Irshad, Tehran, 1347/1968, published to commemorate the 1400th anniversary according to the lunar calendar of the prophecy of Muhammad (blessings be upon him and his household). The paper is translated from Farsi into English by Dr Karim Aghili.

The second paper is entitled "The Prophet Muhammad as portrayed in Nahj al-Balaghah". In this paper Mohammad Javad Shomali has attempted to illustrate an image of the Prophet Muhammad based on the words of Imam Ali b. Abi Talib. Since Imam Ali was brought up by the Prophet Muhammad himself and stayed with him all his life, his account of the character of the Prophet is of utmost importance. This is in addition to the Imam's own insight, piety and knowledge that make his position among all Muslims very special and his view about the Prophet particularly significant.

The third paper is entitled "the Prophet Muhammad from the Shi'a Perspective". In this paper Dr Muhammad Legenhausen gives an account of the Prophet Muhammad based on the Quran, hadiths, Shi'a kalam, Islamic philosophy and 'irfan (mysticism). He ends his paper by elaborating on the idea of absolute prophethood.

The fourth paper is entitled "Subjects of Love According to the Prophet Muhammad". Dr Abbas Ali Shameli studies a well-known hadith of the Prophet Muhammad about three things from this world that are made lovable to him. Referring to different versions of the hadith narrated in Shi'i and Sunni sources, Dr Shameli adopts a theological approach to the hadith and explains the reason behind each object. He ends the paper with a brief review of Ibn Arabi's mystical interpretation of this hadith.

The fifth paper is entitled "Pearls of Wisdom: A Selection of Hadiths from the Prophet Muhammad" and in it, Husayn Naghavi refers to fifty hadiths from the Prophet Muhammad that relate to different aspects of human life.

I would like to thank all who have contributed to this volume and pray for their success in both their personal and academic lives. I thank Mrs. Saajida Rhemtulla for editing and proofreading the whole work and making valuable comments. I would also like to thank Hujjatul-Islam wa'l-Muslimin Moezzi, the Director of the Islamic Centre of England for his support and encouragement. And last, but not the least, I thank God the Almighty for His guidance and favour upon us in the past and present.

Mohammad Ali Shomali

August 2009

A Glimpse of the Character Traits of the Prophet Muhammad

Ayatollah Sayyid Abu'l-Fadl Mujtahid Zanjani

Translated from the Persian by Karim Aghili

Introduction

Since the foundation of Islam up to the present day, biographers, historians and narrators of tradition have gathered details about the life of the holy Prophet in thousands of their works and compilations and have thus placed rich and valuable sources of information within the reach of researchers. However, in most of these works, the characteristics of the life of the Prophet have not been categorized in an orderly manner but are instead, rather disorderly. Therefore, it is not easy to become acquainted with these characteristics. In addition, as most of these works have been written in Arabic, they are inaccessible to those who are unfamiliar with this language. The technological lifestyle of the present age further aggravates the situation because rather than providing more time and opportunity for human beings, against all expectations, it has caused time constraints and has prevented people from spending time reading these detailed works. For this reason, and with regards to the significance of the topic in hand, the writer of this article, while acknowledging his poor knowledge, will seek to place within the reach of readers, a brief summary of the way of life of the Prophet. Efforts have been made to use information that is in conformity with what is unanimously agreed upon by, or widely known among the historians and the reliable narrators of tradition.

"If you cannot drink [all] the ocean's water,

take a sip of it to quench your thirst." (Rumi)

1. Childhood

Muhammad's father, 'Abdullah, died at a young age away from his birthplace and kinsfolk, without knowing that his wife was expecting and that he was leaving behind a precious legacy for the world of humanity. 'Abdullah was the most beloved of the sons of 'Abd al-Muttalib, who sacrificed one hundred camels for him and distributed the meat among the needy. 'Abdullah did not return from a trade journey to Syria. He died in Medina a few days after falling ill and was buried in the house of a member of the tribe of Banu Najjar [*Dār al-Nābighah*].

'Abd al-Muttalib was very upset at this tragic loss but his deep grief and heartbreak was somewhat alleviated by his newborn grandson, the only memory of 'Abdullah left to him. He found peace of mind in him and came to love the child ardently. On the seventh day after his birth he named him Muhammad (the praised one). This name was rare among the Arabs of the time. It is reported that upon being asked why 'Abdul-Muttalib had named his grandson in this way, he replied,

> "I did so with the desire that my grandson would be praised by God in Heaven and by men on earth."[1]

It seemed as if he inwardly knew his grandson's destiny, and the name Muhammad, which befitted his grandson, had been inspired.

It was the general custom of the Arabs who lived in towns to send their children away to Bedouin wet nurses. It was believed that growing up in the free and healthy surroundings of the desert would be deeply effective in aiding the physical and mental development as well as the eloquent speech and gallantry of children. Therefore, 'Abd al-Muttalib entrusted the young Muhammad (S) into the care of Halimah, daughter of 'Abdullah ibn Harith, who belonged to the noble tribe of the Banu Sa'd.

Muhammad (S) lived for about six years in this tribe and with the passage of time, he developed well both physically and mentally. He became more mature than others of the same age in every respect. He was cleaner, more joyful and more magnanimous than all the other children. At the age of six, Halimah took Muhammad (S) to his mother. This noble lady was still grieving the death of her beloved husband and thinking of her only orphaned child brought more sadness to her tender heart.

In order to show her fidelity, to relieve her deep sorrow and to revisit the grave of her husband, who had left her a few days after their marriage, she set out for the long journey to Medina (at that time known as *Yathrib*), accompanied by her beloved son. Muhammad (S) went with her so that he too could shed tears over the grave of his father and sympathize with his mother, since he had already been deprived of the caress, smiles and care of his father. Amina stayed in Medina for a whole month, and everyday she would sit at the grave of her husband and relieve her burning heart through her tears. This painful sight was imprinted on the memory of Muhammad (S). Later, during the emigration, while he was passing through the lanes of Medina he recognized a house and said that he had been in it with his mother and it was there that his father lay buried.[2]

The deep grief and heavy blow suffered by her at the early stage of her married life led to Aminah's premature death. On her journey back to Mecca, she fell ill and died at a place called Abwā'. Muhammad (S) was now completely orphaned. Upon the death of his mother whose presence, love and care he was in need of, the six year-old boy's tender and sensitive heart became mournful. His subtle spirit was overcome with an unforgettable grief. It has been recorded that after fifty-five years, during the journey for performing the compensatory or lesser pilgrimage (*'umrat al-qaḍā*), Muhammad (S) passed the grave of his mother, where he stopped and wept so much that those present there were also moved to tears. It is said that it was the memory of the affection of his mother that moved him to tears. [3]

2. Under the Care of 'Abd al-Mutallib

Umm Ayman (or Barakah, a notable African woman who was esteemed highly by the noble Prophet), took him to Medina and left him with 'Abd al-Muttalib. Seeing the child bereft of his mother as well aroused 'Abd al-Muttalib's pity and affection and his love for his grandson increased. He loved him more than all of his own children[4] and never left him. Even when an assembly of the Quraysh nobles was held in the Sacred Mosque (*masjid al-harām*), 'Abd al-Muttalib would sit in a prominent place and let Muhammad (S) sit on the couch and whenever his uncles wanted to drive the child away from the seat of his father, he would prevent them from doing so saying, "Leave my son alone". He foretold, based on his inspiration or insight, that his grandson would have a very bright future. [5] However, even the amount of love and affection shown by his grandfather could never fill the gap caused by the loss of his parents. Muhammad (S) most often displayed his grief within the context of the following moral lesson:

> "Stroke the heads of the orphans and honour those who are away from their homes, because I became an orphan as a child, and as an adult, I became afflicted with the pain of being away from home". [6]

In order to encourage others to help this underprivileged group in society, he said,

> "Whoever looks after an orphan and brings him up until he is an adult will be next to me in heaven".[7]

It was providentially foreordained that this new stage of his life, in which he almost found peace of mind, would not last long. When he was eight years of age, his grandfather died, and Muhammad (S) experienced more grief. He escorted the dead body of 'Abd al-Muttalib weeping silently.[8] The Prophet had thus been endowed with the ability to tolerate a high degree of hardship in order to prepare him for the hardships and sufferings that would occur during his prophetic mission. It was necessary that the Prophet should taste grief and pain from his early childhood so that he could develop a forbearing and patient spirit.

3. Under the Care of Abu Talib

'Abd al-Muttalib embraced the Prophet on his deathbed, crying, and turned to his eldest son Abu Talib, who was to become his father's successor and the chief of the Hashim clan. Abu Talib was a highly respected man of the Arab tribes. 'Abd al-Muttalib gave him his final instruction, saying,

> "Remember, my son, that after me you should take care of and support this only gem who was bereft of his father's presence and who did not enjoy the affection of his mother. Protect him as your own and keep him away from any harm. I do not know of anyone from among the Arabs like his father who died in the prime of his life, away from his home and without fulfilling his young desires. His mother, who passed away in deep distress, frustration and sorrow, also left him alone. Will you accept my last will?"

Abu Talib responded,

> "Yes father, and I call upon God as a Witness."

He then put his hand over his father's and made a pledge of allegiance to him to which 'Abd al-Muttalib replied,

> "Now it has become easy for me to die".

To bid him a final farewell, he held his grandson close to his chest, smelt and kissed him and breathed his last breath.[9]

Thereafter the courageous Abu Talib, in order to preserve the veneration of his nephew and to protect him, made every effort possible for more than forty years, until he also breathed his last. He protected Muhammad (S) with bravery, sincerity and unique self-sacrifice. His wife Fatimah, who was also one of the lionhearted women of the Quraysh, nursed him together with her husband, and out of her motherly affection (which the holy Prophet never forgot), she spared nothing to provide him with more comfort than her own children. His behaviour in the house of Abu Talib attracted everyone's attention and before long he was well-loved by the whole family.[10] Unlike other children of his age who appeared dishevelled with messy hair and dirty eyes, the Prophet always made his hair tidy and kept his face clean. He had the appearance of an adult who lived in comfort. He was not greedy for food in the least. The children sharing food with him, as is the custom of children, ate hurriedly and sometimes snatched morsels from each other, but he contented himself with little food and avoided eating greedily.[11] He was magnanimous beyond his years and under all circumstances. Sometimes, as soon as he got up, he would go to the well of Zam Zam and drink a few sips of water from that well. Then, when he was called to have a meal in the morning, he would say that he did not feel hungry and did not want to eat.[12] He never complained of feeling hungry or thirsty during his childhood or adulthood.[13] Abu Talib always let him sleep beside his own bed. He narrates,

> "One day, I told him [the Prophet] to take off his clothes and go to bed. I sensed that he did not like my order but as he did not like to refuse, he said, 'Uncle, turn away from me so that I can take off my shirt.' I was very surprised at this. I never heard any lie nor saw any indecent act or laughter from him. He did not like childish games and enjoyed seclusion and loneliness, and he was always humble."[14]

4. Working as a Shepherd

Once, while he was living under the care of Halimah, Muhammad (S) asked her, "Where do my brothers go?" Halimah replied that the other men were taking their sheep to the pasture. The Prophet then said, "I will be with them from today onwards."[15] At the age of seven, he was seen carrying clay in the folds of his long shirt to help Abdullah ibn Jud'an in building houses. He was not seen spending a single day in idleness throughout his life. When praying, he always said: "O God, I take refuge in you from idleness, laziness and abjectness."[16] He encouraged Muslims to work and said,

> "Worship consists of seventy parts, the best of which is to earn a livelihood through lawful means. The supplication of one who sits at home and who asks God for provision without working is not answered." [17]

And,

> "If any of you carries a pack of firewood on his shoulder, it will be better than to ask someone else who may give it or may not."[18]

Perhaps, it was because of this very interest in work and also because he did not like to live among the family of Abu Talib without taking any responsibility and contributing to their means of livelihood, that he started shepherding the sheep of Abu Talib.[19]

Furthermore, from his early childhood, the Prophet liked open spaces and vast deserts, and the idea of seclusion had been gaining strength in his mind. It was as if he had been inspired to move away from the confines and hustle and bustle of the city so that he could reflect on the world of creation insightfully and consider its parts precisely. The power of thought spreads and flourishes well in open spaces, like light waves that do not encounter any obstacles. On the other hand, looking after simple animals, protecting them from the harm of wild animals and precipices and preventing them from fighting with one another was good experience for the Prophet's future mission. The reason was that he would face ignorant, misguided and headstrong people and would have to save them from the dangerous situations that they were caught in. Before him, Moses and David had been shepherds for periods of time as well.[20] Being a shepherd therefore, was not a shameful profession.

5. Leading the Trade Caravan

The Prophet made some trade journeys to Syria and the Yemen. His first journey was made when he accompanied his uncle Abu Talib to Busra, where he learned the techniques of trading. On his last journey, he was hired by Khadijah, whose merchandise he took to Syria and returned with a great profit. He always observed justice and equity while he was trading and avoided telling lies and fraud, which was the practiced by many tradesmen.

Muhammad (S) was never strict in his business dealings with others. Sa'ib ibn al-Sa'ib relates,

> "During the age of ignorance, I was his [the Prophet's] trade partner, and I found him the best of the partners in every respect. He neither argued with anyone nor was he obstinate and nor did he blame anything on his partner."[21]

He became so well-known for his truthfulness and honesty that everyone who knew him acknowledged his trustworthiness and called him Muhammad *al-amin* (the trustworthy).[22] During the prophetic mission, when the Quraysh rose to oppose him, they nevertheless still entrusted their goods to him. An example of his trustworthiness can be seen when he emigrated to Medina and ordered Ali to stay in Mecca primarily so that he could return the things that people had entrusted to him to their respective owners. He considered truthfulness and trustworthiness to be the basis of life and said:

> "These two [virtues] have been confirmed and emphasized in all the teachings of the prophets and apply to anyone who is entrusted with a task."

He also said,

> "Each one of you is a guardian and is responsible for what he is entrusted with."[23]

6. Towards the Oppressed

During the age of ignorance, there was no legal system or authority that could safeguard the limits of individual rights or to which one could appeal for litigation and adjudication. Excluding those who relied on their own power, influence or tribal partisanship, the rest of the people were subject to all kinds of transgressions, against life, property and family. A savage and barbarous temper and the law of the jungle were dominant. In the city of Mecca, the situation was very chaotic. Strangers were especially mistreated. Their belongings were often snatched in public and sometimes, they themselves were taken captive. Of course, among this unbridled multitude, there were a small number of people who had not totally abandoned human virtues, and there were traces of emotion, mercy and chivalry in their hearts. Naturally, they were annoyed at and exhausted with this abnormal situation. One day, an event occurred that significantly moved them, and in response to their dissatisfaction and the injustice they saw, they took some positive steps.

A stranger from the Zubayd tribe came to sell his merchandise in Mecca. 'Âs ibn Wa'il, one of the chieftains of the Quraysh, acquired the entire amount but paid nothing in return. As a result of this, Zubayd approached several influential leaders of the Quraysh to no avail. They refused to listen to him. In despair, he went to the top of Mount Abu Qubays and pleaded for justice in a loud voice, saying,

> "O family of Fahr! [Fahr was the ancestor of the Quraysh, that is, Quraysh himself. He was the man who the entire tribe was related to and was well-known for his chivalry.] I am a stranger in your city and have not yet performed the rituals of *'Umra* (the lesser pilgrimage). I have been shown no respect and my goods have been unjustly possessed. Where are the brave men who can come to my rescue and safeguard my right?"

The sigh of the oppressed man resounded in the air and moved the hearts of the dissatisfied people of Mecca. Muhammad (S), accompanied by his uncle Zubayr ibn 'Abd al-Muttalib, rose up and with the help of some of the leaders of the clans of the Quraysh assembled in the house of 'Abdullah ibn Jud'an al-Taymi. Together, they made a pact for the repression of acts of lawlessness and the restoration of justice to the weak and oppressed.

Then all the members of the covenant approached 'Âs ibn Wa'il together. He could not resist the angry people moved by injustice and was forced to yield and to return the merchandise of the man.[24] The holy Prophet remembered this event afterwards and said,

> "I was present when the covenant was made in the house of 'Abdullah ibn Jud'an, and I will not break that covenant under any circumstance. Even right now I am ready to participate in such a pact."[25]

From Muhammad (S)'s point of view, all the members of a society are duty-bound to resist oppressors and should not be content as onlookers. He has also been quoted to have said,

> "Help your brother whether he is the oppressor or the oppressed one."

When his companions asked him how they should help an oppressor he replied.

> "By preventing him from oppressing others."[26]

7. Towards His Family

Despite Prophet Muhammad's youthful vigour and vivacity he was never influenced by his urges and desires, as a consequence of the virtues of chastity and magnanimity that he possessed. Before his marriage, he was never seen with Khadijah nor was it ever heard or said that he was intimate with women. For instance, even after he emigrated to Medina, in his old age, he married several women, but each marriage was based on expediency. If he had intended to seek gratification, he would not have married older women. It was very easy for him to marry beautiful girls to obtain pleasure, but he condemned and cursed those who considered marriage as a means of obtaining pleasure only.[27]

The Prophet's first wife was Khadijah, daughter of Khuwaylid ibn al-Asadi, who belonged to a well-known family. She herself was regarded to be the First Lady of the Quraysh. She was endowed with chastity and honesty, and for this distinction, she was called al-Tahirah (the pure one).[28] She was one of the wealthiest traders in Mecca. She had turned down several noblemen of the Quraysh who proposed marriage to her, believing that they were after her wealth. The well-known moral virtues of Muhammad (S) the Trustworthy attracted the attention of Khadijah. She found in him the qualities that she had long been searching for and married him. Unlike most marriages prevalent at the time, their marriage did not occur out of love for position, wealth, beauty, financial and material gain, or for ostentation. Rather, it was a marriage based on moral homogeneity, love of virtue, spiritual union and mutual affection, giving it permanence. This marital union played an extremely effective and useful role in the propagation of the call of Islam and the encouragement of the messenger of God.

Khadijah, a virtuous and self-sacrificing woman, always shared her husband's pain and comfort and consoled him in the face of hardships. She gave away all her wealth to the needy for the exaltation of the proclamation of *Tawhid* (the Oneness of God). Khadijah was the first woman who converted to Islam and prayed behind her husband. The Blessed Prophet married no other woman as long as she was alive. After her death he re-married and treated all his wives kindly and justly without giving preference to one over the other. Whenever the Prophet intended to go on a journey, he would draw lots among his wives and would take with him the one to whom the lot fell.[29] He was not morally rough but especially kind and tolerant. He tolerated the bad-temperedness and foul language of his wives, even when some of them were so bold as to disclose his private secrets and annoy him by plotting and colluding, to the point where Qur'anic verses were sent down admonishing and reprimanding them.[30]

After the wars with Banu Naḍir and Banu Qurayzah (the two Jewish tribes), some of his wives fantasized about an aristocratic and luxurious life and demanded jewellery, knowing that the treasures of the Jews were now in possession of the blessed Prophet. The Prophet, who did not want to sacrifice social justice for the whims of his wives and let the public Muslim treasury be used privately, refused to accept their demand and paid no attention to their rough words. Abu Bakr and 'Umar, who were informed of this matter, were determined to punish their respective daughters 'A'ishah and Hafsah but the blessed Prophet prevented them from doing so.[31] He just contented himself with keeping away from them. After one month, it was ordered, based on the Qur'anic verses revealed on the occasion, that he should let his wives choose one of two alternatives: if either of them was still interested in being his wife, she should abandon seeking an increase in wealth, live a simple and contented life and be hopeful of more reward. However, if either of them preferred the luxuries and glitter of this world, then the Prophet should release her in a fair manner.[32]

The blessed Prophet elevated the status of women to the level of full human beings who had the right to independent possession of their lives and property. He always, even in the last moments of his life, recommended getting along with one's wife; that is, observing the exigencies of a woman's primordial nature and exemplified this in the following way:

> "A woman is like a rib which will break if you try to straighten it. You can benefit from it if it remains as it was made (by Allah)."[33]

The order of creation and the limits of human primordial nature cannot be changed, and some things that can be done by men cannot be done by women, and within the order of creation each one has his/her own position and talents. The Prophet emphasized that women should be treated kindly and said,

> "All people have both good and bad qualities and a husband should not just consider the bad qualities of his wife and hate her, because when he is displeased with one bad quality in her, he becomes pleased with that one which is good and these two points should be considered together."[34]

Prophet Muhammad also cursed those who fail to struggle for the comfort of their family, saying,

> "One who neglects his family and leaves them alone is deprived of the mercy of God."[35]

He treated his children kindly explaining that, "our children are an integral part of us." He was diligent in rearing his children and taught them the etiquette of Islam. He used to say,

> "Fatimah is part of me, and she is my heart and soul, and whoever offends her offends me."[36]

And,

> "Hasan and Husayn are from me and I am from them."

When the Prophet would go into prostration, Hasan and Husayn would climb on his shoulders and he would either prolong his prostration until they got down, or slowly put them down and rise from prostration. He embraced them and kissed their cheeks and faces. One day, one of the people present with the Prophet saw this and commented, "We never kiss our children." The Prophet responded,

> "What can I do for you if God has removed from your hearts the feeling of compassion?"

Another day, when he sat Hasan on his knee and kissed the child's face, Aqra' ibn Habis said,

> "I have got ten children, and I have never kissed any of them.'

The Prophet looked at him and said,

> "One who has no compassion for others is not entitled to compassion (from God)."[37]

The Prophet not only caressed his own children but he was also affectionate towards the children of others and embraced and greeted them.[38] Furthermore, the blessed Prophet's love and affection did not stop there. He also embraced his servants. Anas ibn Malik narrates,

> "I served the Prophet, peace be upon him, in his house day and night for ten years and he never said to me 'why did you do that?' after I had done something or 'why did you not do that?' after I had neglected to do something. He never said a word of contempt to me".[39]

In short, he treated his family kindly, not strictly or severely and said,

> "The best of you is he who is the best to his family, and I am the best among you to my family".[40]

8. Towards the Slaves

Slavery is one of the hideous habits of man and is indicative of his cruelty. It has been prevalent since the early history of mankind, gradually becoming a part of the rights of masters and of indisputable social principles. As such it has permeated all human societies to the extent that even the intellectuals and scholars of many nations considered it expedient and right. In these civilizations not only were there no steps taken to abolish it but there were also no steps taken to amend it. The Greek philosophers believed that two types of human beings were created: the free and the slaves, and that the latter were created to serve the former. Aristotle considered the system of slavery to be one of the necessities of human society. He said that with regards to work, when more manpower is needed, the government should use slaves, but attention should be paid to the improvement of their lives.

The blessed Prophet understood with his mature reason and sound conscience that human beings are alike in terms of their primordial nature and natural talents. He knew that they all possess souls, wills, sentiments and emotions. He also understood that differences in race, colour, language, nationality and even the privilege of piety and knowledge cannot be the cause of discrimination against them and their rights. Why do some human individuals enslave others, and deprive them of their freedom and due privileges? The Prophet was well aware that removing a thousand-year-long idea that had penetrated deeply into the minds of both masters and slaves would not be possible, except by changing social modes of thought. If a code was legislated without an executive backing or enforcement guarantee from within the souls of the masters and the slaves, this deep-rooted class system would never be abolished. After all, the masters considered the blatant injustice to be part and parcel of their rights.

The slaves too, by force of habit had gradually become too weak to exercise their willpower and were not able to act freely. As a result of their total lack of a sense of freedom and free living, they came to believe that their right to live was confined to the very cruel situation in which they were caught. Therefore, the social situation had to be improved in parallel with the gradual social growth. Much thought and wisdom was needed when taking measures to put this into effect.

As an initial step, the Prophet advised the masters and the slaves to regard one another as brothers on a number of occasions. He began convincing them that they were all of the same race and were created from clay.[41] He said,

> "Whites have no natural privilege over Blacks, and the worst of people in the sight of God are slave traders.[42] Slaves are your brothers. They have been put under your command and they have their own rights. You should feed them of what you eat and dress them of what you wear. Do not ask them to do things beyond their capacity and help them to do things.[43] When you call them, call them politely and do not say, 'My slave' or 'my slave-girl'. Rather, you should say, 'my lad', 'my lass' or 'my boy'. All your men and all your women are servants of God, and He is the True Master of all."[44]

This expressive and appropriate logic, which emanated from the depths of the heart of a true humanitarian in the form of a heavenly message, played a major role in breaking the arrogance of masters, in obliterating the sense of inferiority from the hearts of the slaves, in the intellectual transformation of many people and in creating doubt about something that was considered an indisputable principle for centuries. Naturally, it made people reconsider their situations and they gradually came to the conclusion that a brother should not subjugate his fellow brother.

Thereafter, through his practical steps, the blessed Prophet paved the way for the freeing of the slaves, either by encouraging the people to do so and promising them a reward: their sins would be expiated and their repentance would be accepted; or the slaves could be emancipated through redemption (repurchase) so that they would pay their masters a certain amount of money out of their wages by instalments, or that it would be paid from the public Muslim treasury (*bayt al-māl*) until they were free.

In this way, the Prophet blocked almost all the roads leading to slavery so that it would gradually die out. He took the lead, demonstrating by practical example, and freed his slave Zayd ibn Haritha, who his wife Khadijah had presented to him. Furthermore, in order to erase the sense of inferiority and servitude from Zayd's mind, he called him his 'adopted son' in public. As soon as Zayd reached the age of puberty, the Prophet gave his cousin in marriage to him, in order to abolish racial superiority on which the world in those days, especially the world of Arab tribalism, relied heavily. Thus, the Prophet founded the principle of equality.

9. Cleanliness

As previously mentioned, the blessed Prophet was interested in cleanliness from his early childhood and was unique in observing cleanliness of the body and clothes. In addition to observing the manners of *wuḍu* (ablution), he washed and bathed himself on most days and encouraged both of these as acts of worship. He washed his hair which fell to his ear lobes with Lote tree leaves (*sidr*) and combed and rubbed violet oil in it. He perfumed himself with musk and ambergris incense so that his scent could be smelled wherever he passed. He cleaned his teeth with a natural toothbrush (*miswāk*) carefully, several times a day, especially before sleeping and after waking up. His white garment, which reached below his knees, was always clean.

Before and after eating, he used to wash his hands and mouth and would avoid eating bad-smelling herbs and/or vegetables. An ivory comb, a collyrium for the eyes, a container, a pair of scissors, a mirror and a *miswāk* (a natural toothbrush) were always part of his luggage wherever he went. His house was always clean, despite its simplicity and lack of luxury. He emphasised that rubbish should be taken out during the day and should not be left till night. His physical cleanliness was in harmony with his sacred spiritual purity. He advised his companions and followers to keep their heads, bodies, garments and houses clean and he especially persuaded them to wash and perfume themselves on Fridays so that they would not smell bad while attending the Friday prayer.[45]

He further ordered his followers not to relieve themselves near graves, beside rivers or in the shade of trees. He emphasised that care should be taken not to pollute water to the extent that even while washing, it was better to wash outside the water rather than entering it.[46]

10. Manners of Social Interaction

The blessed Prophet was cheerful and bright in public but had a sad and meditative expression when he was in private. He never stared at anyone's face and used to look down more often than he raised his head. He was careful to greet everyone first, even the slaves and children. He often used to sit on his knees and would not stretch his legs in the presence of others. Whenever he entered an assembly, he used to sit in the nearest vacant spot and never allowed anyone to stand up for him or make room for him. While being addressed, he did not interrupt the speaker and treated his associate in such a manner that the associate would go away thinking himself to be the dearest person to the Messenger of God. He did not speak unnecessarily. He spoke slowly and clearly and never used bad language. He was a perfect model of modesty and shyness. He never got annoyed at anyone's behaviour but on occasion, annoyance might appear on his face. He never used to complain or object. He frequently visited the sick and participated in funeral processions. He did not allow anyone to speak against anyone else except when pleading for justice.

In one incident, a group of Jews came to the blessed Prophet and said, "as-Sām-u-'Alaykum" (death be upon you), whereupon the Prophet replied, "Wa 'alaikum". 'A'isha understood their meaning and cursed them but the Prophet told her, "'A'isha, do not do that, for God does not like the use of harsh words".[47]

11. Forgiveness

The Prophet always overlooked the maltreatment and disrespect shown towards him. He did not hold a grudge against anyone and never sought to take revenge. His powerful spirit, which transcended passiveness and psychic complexes, preferred forgiveness over revenge. His sensitivity to adversities did not go beyond grief. In the Battle of Uhud, despite the level of cruelty and disrespect carried out on the dead body of Hamzah ibn 'Abd al-Muttalib, which hurt the Prophet and saddened him deeply, he did not retaliate against the dead of the Quraysh. Even afterwards, when he gained access to the perpetrators of that cruelty including Hind, the wife of Abu Sufyan, he did not seek revenge. In fact, when Abu Qutadah al-Ansari was about to curse them, the Prophet prevented him from doing so.[48]Another similar incident took place after the victory at Khaybar, when a group of the Jews who had surrendered sent poisonous food to the Prophet. The Prophet was informed of their attempt on his life, but forgave them.[49] On yet another occasion, he also forgave a Jewish woman who was the perpetrator of a plot to feed him poison.[50]

'Abdullah ibn Ubayy, the leader of the hypocrites, who had been granted immunity by acknowledging the *Shahada* (the Muslim declaration of belief in the oneness of God and the acceptance of Muhammad (S) as his prophet), and who had been nurturing hostility in his heart toward the blessed Prophet, thought that with the emigration of the Prophet to Medina, his governance would come to an end. He was colluding with the hostile Jews and was active in the defamation of the Prophet, provocation of hostility towards him and rumour-mongering about him. It was he who, at the Battle of Bani al-Mustaliq, said,

> "When we return to Medina, those with honour will drive out those who are dishonorable, that is the emigrants (*muhājirin*)".

The companions of the holy Prophet who had a deep-rooted hatred for 'Abdullah ibn Ubayy frequently asked the Prophet to punish him. However, not only did the Prophet not permit them to do so, but he also treated 'Abdullah with the utmost tolerance. When 'Abdullah ibn Ubayy was sick, the Prophet visited him. He attended his funeral and prayed over his dead body as well.[51]

It has also been narrated that a group of hypocrites once plotted to kill the Prophet while he was on his way back from the Battle of Tabuk. They planned to terrify his camel and thereby make him fall into the valley as he passed along the mountain road. They had covered their faces, but the Prophet identified them. Nevertheless, he did not divulge their names in spite of the insistence of his companions and overlooked their punishment.[52]

12. The Limits of Law

The Prophet readily pardoned any mistreatment of his own scared person, but he never disregarded or overlooked those who violated the limits of the law. When it came to administering justice and punishing the violators of it, he was not lenient at all because the laws of justice safeguard social security and are crucial to the very existence of society. These laws should therefore not be trifled with by whimsical people otherwise society would be sacrificed for the individual. In the year of the conquest of Mecca, a woman belonging to the famous tribe of

Makhzum committed theft and her crime was legally confirmed. Her relatives, who were still under the influence of the pre-Islamic class system, felt that the punishment due for the woman would disgrace them too. They tried to influence the holy Prophet so that the sentence for theft might not be passed. Usama ibn Zaid, who was loved by the holy Prophet, was selected to intercede for her so that the punishment might be overlooked by the Prophet. As he was about to attempt to intercede, the Prophet said,

> "Do you try to intercede for somebody in a case connected with God's Prescribed Punishments?"

Usama became aware of his error, apologized and asked God for forgiveness. Then the Prophet got up and delivered a sermon in which he explained the matter in the following way;

> "What destroyed the nations preceding you was that if a noble among them stole, they would forgive him, and if a poor person among them stole, they would inflict God's Legal Punishment on him. By Allah in whose Hands is my life, I will not be lenient in administering justice to anyone, even if the criminal be my nearest relative."[53]

Moreover, Muhammad (S) did not exclude himself or consider himself above the law. One day, he went to the mosque and ascended the pulpit from where he addressed the people. During his speech he said,

> "The Most High God has sworn that He will not overlook any unjust or oppressive acts so in God's name I beseech whoever has suffered an injustice at the hands of Muhammad to rise up and take his revenge, for retribution in this world is more desirable to me than retribution in the next world, in the presence of God's angels and the prophets."

Sawada ibn Qays then stood up saying,

> "May my mother and father be sacrificed for you oh Messenger of God. When you were coming from Tā'if, I came to greet you and you were riding upon your she-camel with your stick in hand and when you raised it to strike your camel you struck me in the abdomen. I do not know whether you did it intentionally or unintentionally."

The Prophet replied,

> "God forbid that I should do such a thing intentionally."

He then ordered for his stick to be brought to him and asked Sawada to return the strike, like for like. Sawada rose and approached the Prophet, but when he reached him he began to kiss his body. The Prophet asked him,

> "Are you taking your revenge or granting your pardon?"

Whereupon Sawada said,

> "I am granting my pardon."

The Prophet then prayed for him, saying,

> "May God forgive you too!"[54]

Such was the behaviour of this religio-political leader who was providentially bestowed with full power to administer justice and protect the law.

13. Worship

From very early on in life, when he tended sheep at a place called al-Ajyād, the Prophet cherished seclusion and solitude and spent hours contemplating in the retreat of the desert. He was used to spend long hours meditating and speculating on all aspects of creation around him. He had been in a totally different world from that of his tribe and had never attended their entertainment and amusement gatherings. Furthermore, he did not participate in the pagan ceremonies, nor did he contaminate his hands and mouth with the sacrificial meat offered to the idols.[55] He quickly completed his contemplative journey through the first stage of belief; the Oneness of God (*Tawhid*). That is, he had negated, through reason and contemplation, all but the monotheistic God. He hated the idols and used to say, "I hate nothing more than these idols".[56] In order to pass through the second stage of the proclamation of the Oneness of God (*Tawhid*), the stage of affirmation, his God-given lofty spirit and flowing thought soared high above the visible world. Beyond the boundaries of the visible world and in an amazing, yet fleetingly transient phenomena, he contemplated the Omnipotent and Everlasting Creator. He used to acknowledge this in his heart:

> "Lo! I have turned my face toward Him Who created the heavens and the earth, as one by nature upright, and I am not of the idolaters." (6:79)

From then on, his attachment to seclusion and retreat increased and he found Mount Hirā an appropriate setting for his purpose. He spent most of his time there and every now and again went into retreat and secluded himself for several consecutive nights, with little provision, solely to worship the One God.[57] Regretfully, his manner of worship while he was in the cave on Mount Hirā has been passed over and therefore silenced in history so very little can be said about it. No one else had access to the retreat and it is not known whether the Prophet knelt down or raised his hands during supplication or if he prostrated himself during the moments he spent in the cave. He might have done all of these. In any case, he had comprehended the reality of worship. In truth, worship has no meaning other than self-negation, attention, resignation (*riḍā*) and submission (*taslim*) to God, the Exalted. After the start of his prophetic mission, the archangel Gabriel taught him the rituals of ablution and prayer as they are laid down in Islamic Law (*Shari'ah*), and from then on he performed the prayer with the same conditions (*shurut*) and essential components (*arkān*) as are observed now, including the awareness or presence of heart.

The Prophet used to spend the greater part of each night in prayer, supplication and communion (*munājāt*) to the extent that his feet were often swollen due to prolonged standing. He considered worship to be a duty of the servant, and he performed it enthusiastically. He did not worship God in the hope of gaining reward or out of fear of punishment. Those who were heedless of his states would say to him sympathetically, "Why do you do this while you are free from all sins?" And he would reply,

"Should I not be a thankful servant?"[58]

In addition to the month of Ramaḍn and the greater part of Sha'ban, the Prophet used to fast on every alternate day throughout the rest of the year.[59] He would retreat in the mosque for the last ten days of the month of Ramaḍan.[60] On the other hand, he was lenient with regards to others. He would say,

> "It is sufficient for you to fast three days in every month. Do as many deeds as you are capable of doing. The deed most liked by God is one to which the doer adheres constantly, even if it is small". [61]

Although he made the correctness or excellence of some acts of worship conditional, depending on specific spatio-temporal characteristics, he generally had a broad view of the acts of worship and did not restrict worshipping God to a specific place or to certain ceremonies or to the direction of certain individuals. He considered everywhere on earth a *masjid* (a place for prostration), considered all servants able to connect with God without the mediation of anyone, and considered every good deed an act of worship on the condition that the act *per se* was legitimate and imbued with sincere intention. The blessed Prophet made this clear in the early years of his prophetic mission when the order of migration to Medina was issued for the purpose of laying the foundation of Islam by declaring,

> "He whose migration is to seek the pleasure of God and His Messenger, his migration is to God and His Messenger; but he whose migration is for some worldly thing he might gain, or for a wife he might marry, his migration is to that for which he is migrating."

He based the criterion for judging the correctness of people's acts on the following statement,

> "Actions are judged according to intentions and everyone will be recompensed according to what he intends."[62]

Any act, even a daily activity, that emanates from a sincere intention will be considered an act of worship. If a husband puts a morsel of food in his wife's mouth[63] or has sexual intercourse with his wife to guard his chastity and not allow himself to be contaminated with sin then this is also worship.[64] Where there is no pure intention, then even prayer and fasting will not be rewarded by God, although they may appear justified.

Muhammad (S) also deemed it necessary to preserve equilibrium between the material and the spiritual life and forbade going to extremes. He condemned isolation from social life... but also condemned giving into animal lusts to the same degree. He showed the middle way between the two with his words and actions and prevented those who spent all their time in prayer and fasting and who were negligent of the affairs of worldly life from deviation by reminding them,

> "Your family has a right upon you, your visitor has a right upon you, and your body has a right upon you". [65]

Once, as he was on one of his journeys, some of the companions who were with him were fasting and others were not. Those who were observing fasts fell down on account of weakness. The companions who had not fasted pitched tents and watered the mounts. Seeing this, the Messenger of God said,

> "The breakers of the fast have received the reward today." [66]

In the stillness of the night, he used to spend long hours keeping vigil and offering night prayer and communion but when he was leading the congregational prayer he was always careful of others and would say,

> "When I stand for prayer, I intend to prolong it but on hearing the cries of a child, I cut it short, as I dislike troubling the child's mother."[67]

In another incident, a man was driving two camels used for agricultural purposes, when night fell. He found a person by the name of Mu'adh praying so he made his camel kneel and joined Mu'adh in prayer. The latter recited *Surat al-Baqarah* (the Chapter of the Cow) and, due to the length of the surah, the traveling man separated himself from the congregation and performed his prayer on his own. Mu'adh was informed of this, and remarked that the man was a hypocrite. When the remark was conveyed to the man, he was upset and went to the Messenger of God to inform him of what Mu'adh had said. Upon hearing what had happened, the Apostle of God became sad and advised Mu'adh,

> "You are scaring people away. It would have been better if you had recited the short chapters, for behind you are the weak, the aged, and the people who have business to attend to. In congregational prayer, you should have a regard for the aged and the weak".[68]

The holy Prophet did not like the raising of voice in supplication as is often done by ostentatious people. While journeying, whenever his companions ascended a high place, they would raise their voices with *Takbir* (glorification of God). The Prophet would come close to them and explain,

> "O people! Don't exert yourselves, for you are not calling on one who is deaf or absent. You are calling the One Who Hears, Who is Near."

And in another version,

> "...and He is nearer to you than the neck of the beast you ride."

And in yet another version,

> "...and He is nearer to you than the jugular vein."[69]

14. Renunciation (*zuhd*)

The Prophet removed all the unnecessary things from his life and set a righteous example. He used to sit on the ground, sleep on a piece of mat made of palm leaves[70] and place a leather cushion filled with palm fibre under his head.[71] His main food was barley, bread and dates. He never ate until he was full and would sometimes have barley-bread for three consecutive days.[72] He broke his fast by eating a small number of dates. When they were not available, he had a few sips of water instead.[73] It has been narrated from 'Ai'shah that sometimes a whole month would pass before the kitchen fire was lit.[74] Muhammad (S) would not criticize the food that he did not like.[75] When he rode, his horse would be unsaddled and he would let someone else ride behind him, should it be convenient for the animal. He used to patch his own garments, cobble his own shoes, milk his own sheep and grind flour himself.[76] In addition, he would help his family with other household chores. And withal, he would go for prayer whenever he heard the call.[77]

Since the goal of the Prophet and his companions was to save humanity from decadence and eradicate idolatry, thus liberating them, how could they be egoists or slaves to their whims? If they had been either of these, it would not have been possible for them to resist three years of hardship in the mountain pass (*shi'b*) of Abu Talib, where the rebels had confined them and denied them access to food and commodities.[78] Similarly, the homeless Meccans, (*ashāb al-suffah* - literally, people of the ledge or portico) could not have lived on the raised platform by the side of the mosque without food, clothing or housing and still resisted. Or in the Batle of Tabuk, it would not have been possible for them to tolerate so much hardship, hunger and thirst in the hot sun of the Arabian Peninsula with patience and forbearance.[79] The true companions continued to live as desert trees with little water. In any case, the high ambitions of just and philanthropic rulers, does not allow them to live in comfort and luxury as long as poverty and hardship exist and people's basic needs have not been met.

That is not to say, of course, that the blessed Prophet was opposed to the acquisition of wealth and the spending of it in lawful and legitimate ways. In fact, he actually supported this:

> "The best assistance to guarding against evil (*taqwā*) is wealth (*ghinā*)."[80]

He considered wealth a means of survival[81] because there is no means more effective than it to further one's objectives.

15. Steadfastness

Muhammad (S) had not only been sent for the guidance of a tribe or a nation but he had also been assigned a universal mission.

> "...that he may be a warner to all the nations" (25:1).[82]

It was necessary that Prophet Muhammad save humanity from the darkness of lust and ignorance, from the worship of animate and inanimate idols, from the despotism and authority of unjust rulers, from the unconditional imitations of the soothsayers and impostors, from the racial and class biases and from material and spiritual poverty. He was also sent to liberate humanity from the many chains that had imprisoned them and had eroded away their souls and bodies, and to abrogate the fake and false criteria that had been accepted for centuries as the means for evaluating habits and character traits and that actually displayed ugliness as beautiful, falsehood as truth and evil as good. In short, he had to destroy a corrupt world and rebuild a new, better world.

In the beginning, when the command for the open call to Islam had not yet been sent down and when only a small number had converted to Islam, the Quraysh thought that the Prophet was also one of *hunafā* (true believers; believers in the fiath of Abraham) and included him with people like Zayd ibn 'Amr ibn Kufayl, 'Uthman ibn Huwayrith and Waraqah ibn Nawfal, who sometimes expressed their opinions on certain matters of theology, but generally did not challenge people. The relationship between those who had converted to Islam and the Prophet was thought to be similar to that of a spiritual master and a novice. Although they caused no inconvenience, some looked upon them as suspicious and annoying.[83] The blessed Prophet was not afraid of praying and/or worshipping in public and was sometimes seen standing in prayer with Ali and his own wife, Khadijah, by the side of the Ka'bah. One day, 'Afif al-Kindi saw them and asked 'Abbas ibn 'Abd al-Muttalib,

> "O 'Abbas, what is this religion? We do not know what this religion is."

'Abbas answered,

> "This is Muhammad ibn 'Abdullah, who claims that Allah called him to be a messenger, and that the treasures of Kisra (Khusraw, the Sassanid Persian Emperor) and Qaysar (Caesar, the Byzantine Emperor) will be opened for him. This is his wife Khadijah, daughter of Khuwaylid, who has believed in him. The youth is his cousin 'Ali ibn Abi Talib".[84]

Three years after this, the Prophet started to open the invitation to Islam under the command of God. His invitation is summarized as follows:

> "I have brought the best of this world and the next. You who worship the idols are in error, because you are following in the footsteps of your fathers and ancestors. They have no power over gain and loss. It is only the Creator of the world Who is Worthy of praise and Who can reward you for your good and evil deeds. I warn you against the path that you have adopted which will lead you to be afflicted with a painful punishment."

These words fell heavily on the ears of the polytheists and upset them. It was his uncle Abu Lahab who first declined the

Prophet's invitation in an aggressive tone. From that day onwards, he and the polytheists rose in opposition and resistance to the advancement of Islam. Their opposition was not just because of their bias in favour of their religious beliefs and sanctities, but also because they saw their whole world threatened by this 'new' religion. Their benefits and social status depended on the situation in Arabia at that time. If a revolution or transformation were to occur, the circumstances would naturally change, and their supremacy and privileges would disappear. The polytheists had installed three hundred and sixty idols in the Ka'bah[85] and each of the Arab tribes worshipped one or more of them. They also considered the Ka'bah to be the house of God and had posed as its guardians and thereby imposed their authority on all of the Arab tribes. They imagined that they had gathered together the deities of heaven and those of the earth so that everybody could worship their own desired object of worship. If they abandoned their idols, they would have to relinquish all the privileges and benefits that had been gained from the frequent visits, offerings and vows of the pilgrims.

Furthermore, haughtiness and jealousy had blinded them and left a profound impact on the intensity of their resistance, as Abu Jahl demonstrated this when he explicitly said,

> "We have competed with the clan of 'Abd Manaf for honour and position and fell behind them on the race field. Now they claim that a prophet has been sent from among them and wish to overtake us. That will never happen".[86]

From then on, the blessed Messenger and his followers were under a lot of pressure and were prevented from performing their religious rites. They were forced to go to a valley outside Mecca where they could pray together without being seen.[87] They were abysmally tormented by the polytheists, who laid them on the ground and put heavy, burning hot stones on their naked backs and chests and tried to force them to abandon the religion of

Muhammad (S) and acknowledge that al-Lāt and al-'Uzzā were their gods.[88] They tied ropes around the necks of the believers and dragged them through the valleys. They dressed their naked bodies in armour and laid them out in the burning sun. Some were beaten, imprisoned and kept hungry and thirsty. The holy Prophet was severely saddened at the extent of the cruelty that was being inflicted on his followers. One day, he happened to see 'Ammar and his mother Sumayyah, who were almost unconscious as a result of the torture they had undergone and said,

> "O family of Yasir, be patient. Your final destination is paradise".

After a while, Yasir was martyred due to the torture and Sumayyah was also martyred by Abu Jahl.[89] This man and woman were the first martyrs for the cause of Islam.

To add insult to injury, the infidels of the Quraysh did not refrain from reviling and insulting the blessed Prophet whenever they met him. One day, while the Prophet was in prostration, 'Uqba bin Abi Mu'ayt placed the abdominal contents (intestines and so on) of a camel on his back, between his shoulders. Allah's Apostle was in prostration and did not lift up his head until his daughter Fatima came and removed them from his back.

On another occasion, while the Prophet was praying in the courtyard of the Ka'ba, the same person came and seized him by the shoulder, twisted his garment round his neck and began choking him brutally. At that time, Abu Bakr came, seized 'Uqba's shoulders and threw him away from the Prophet. The blessed Prophet showed tolerance in the face of this arduous persecution and also enjoined patience upon his followers.

Khabbab ibn Arat narrates:

> "I complained to the Prophet (of the persecution inflicted on us by the infidels) while he was in the

shade of the Ka'bah wall. I said (to him). 'Will you invoke Allah (to help us)?' He sat down with a red face and said, '(A believer among) those who were before you was combed with iron combs so that nothing of his flesh or nerves remained on his bones yet that never made him desert his religion. A saw might have been put over the middle of his head and his head split into two parts, yet all of that would not make him abandon his religion. By Allah! This religion (Islam) will be completed (and triumph).'"[90]

On another occasion, it was said to the Prophet, "Invoke curse upon the polytheists", whereupon he replied,

> "I have not been sent as the invoker of curse, but I have been sent as mercy."[91]

In the face of the steadfastness shown by the blessed Prophet, his opponents from the tribe of Quraysh intensified their obstinacy and decided to nullify his invitation by staining his good name and reputation. He was called a mad man (*majnun*, literally meaning possessed by jinn), a poet, a soothsayer or a magician wherever he went. Rumours were also spread that he alienated father from son or wife from her husband by using witchcraft. They tried to seek out his weak points and during the season of the pilgrimage, they influenced the strangers and pilgrims with nonsensical words to discourage them from communicating with him.[92]

At first, the Quraysh approached the Prophet in a threatening manner. Then they approached Abu Talib, who was Muhammad (S)'s only strong supporter, in order to dissuade him from supporting his nephew, but he did not succumb to them. As soon as they found out that their threats were proving to be ineffective, the Quraysh resorted to bribing. They sent 'Utbah ibn Rabi'ah to him, and he told the Prophet that if he wanted wealth, they would make him the richest man in the country. If he wanted power and leadership, they would make him their ruler as long as he abandoned his call to Islam. However, the Prophet replied, in a decisive and explicit manner deserving of the rank of the divinely-sent prophets,

> "I swear by the Name of God that if they place the sun in my right hand and the moon in my left hand in return for giving up this matter [calling people to Islam], I will never desist until either God makes it triumph or I perish defending it."[93]

In short, neither threat nor bribery nor defamation nor the three-year siege of Shi'b Abi Talib, nor hunger nor deprivation nor homelessness could destroy the Prophet's steadfastness. After twenty-three years of struggle, he accomplished his goal in delivering the message of Islam to the world.

16. Respect for Public Opinion

With regard to the subjects (*mawḍū'*) and rulings (*hukm*) that are determined by definitive revelation (*wahy*) and explicit statements (*nass*), including the divinely legislated acts of worship and transactions, the Prophet did not grant himself, or others the right to intervene and express opinions. This group of rulings should be unconditionally implemented and violating them is regarded as disbelief in God:

> "Whoever does not judge by that which God has revealed: such are disbelievers." (5:44)[94]

However, when it came to subjects pertaining to the individual's life and activity, as long as these were permissible, the individual Muslims were entitled to independent opinion and freedom of action. No one had the right to interfere in the private affairs of others.[95] When it came to society, the Prophet believed that everyone had an equal right to express their opinion. Although his clearly flowing thought and extraordinary intelligence excelled that of others in discerning the public interest, he never behaved in a despotic and/or imperious manner and did not show indifference to public opinion. He always took the opinions of others into consideration while at the same time putting the Qur'anic order into practice and only wanted Muslims to bear this prophetic tendency in mind.

There were three occasions in the Battle of Badr where Prophet Muhammad invited his companions to consult together and asked them to express their opinions. On the first occasion, he consulted his companions as to whether they should fight the Quraysh or leave them alone and return to Medina. All of them preferred to fight so he agreed.[96] Secondly, he consulted his companions about where the camp should be made. At this point he agreed with the advice of Hubab ibn al-Mundhir. And in the third instance, he consulted his companions and followers as to how the captives should be treated. Some were of the view that they should be killed, and others preferred that they should be set free on ransom. The blessed Prophet agreed with the second group.[97]

For the battle of Uhud, the Prophet consulted his companions about the best strategy to follow. He accepted the majority preference to go out of Madinah and meet the armies of the Quraysh rather than remaining inside the fortifications to fight.[98]

At the battle of Ahzab, the Prophet held an urgent consultation as to whether they should draw up their forces and array them outside Medina or defend themselves inside the city. After the consultation, it was agreed that Mount Sal' should be used as the headquarters of the army of Islam and a trench should be dug to act as a barrier to stop the enemy forces advancing and prevent them from attacking.[99]

During the battle of Tabuk, the Roman emperor became scared and frightened when the army of Islam approached the frontier of

Syria. He did not launch an attack because he could not count on his army. At this juncture the Prophet assembled his esteemed officers and, acting on the established Islamic principle of consultation, he asked for their views as to whether they should advance into the territory of the enemy or return to Madina. As a result of this military consultation it was decided that the army of Islam should return to Madina.[100]

It is common knowledge that all Muslims believe in the Prophet's infallibility and do not find any of his deeds objectionable.[101] However, the blessed Prophet was nevertheless tolerant towards criticism even if it was irrelevant and baseless, and he was careful not to place them under suffocating circumstances. Instead, he used to make the critic aware of his error in a quiet and gentle way and by using convincing arguments. He used to abide by the natural law that the Creator of the world has endowed all humans with, the power of thinking and criticizing, and openly acknowledged that this is not exclusive to those who possess influence and power. He did not allow the rights of freedom of expression and criticism to be denied to the people. He particularly ordered his followers to exercise their rights in the face of a ruler who does something against the laws of justice by rejecting and protesting against it.

Once, the Prophet sent out an army to carry out a campaign. He appointed a man from the Ansar as its commander and ordered the soldiers to obey him. During the campaign, the commander became angry with his soldiers and said, "Didn't the Prophet order you to obey me?" They replied in the affirmative. Then he said, "I order you to collect wood and make a fire and then throw yourselves into it." So the soldiers collected wood and made a fire, but just as they were about to throw themselves into it they started having second thoughts. They looked at each other, and some of them said,

> "We followed the Prophet to escape from the fire. We embraced Islam to save ourselves from the 'fire' so why should we enter it now?"

While they were in that state of indecision, the fire went out and with it went their commander's anger. The event was relayed to the Prophet, who said,

> "If they had entered it [the fire] they would never have come out of it [i.e. out of the fire of injustice], for obedience [to someone's orders] is required only when he enjoins what is good." [102]

At the battle of Hunayn, the Prophet deemed it expedient to allocate a large proportion of the booty to the newly converted Meccans. Sa'd ibn 'Ubadah and some of the other Medinite Ansar who were among the foremost warriors, expressed their dissatisfaction with the preference given by the Prophet to the Ansar. When their discontent reached the ears of Muhammad (S), he assembled the disheartened Medinite Ansars together, and with an eloquent and pleasant mode of expression, he made them aware of the causes of his partiality and of their own error. When they heard the Prophet's words, the Ansars present started weeping and apologized to him.[103]

In another incident that occurred after the Battle of Hunayn, a man called Hurqus from the tribe of Banu Tamim, (who later became one of the chiefs of the Kharijites), rebuked the Prophet by saying, "Be just in your distribution O Messenger of Allah." 'Umar ibn Khattab was incensed by this rude remark and asked the Prophet to allow him to behead Hurqus. The Prophet said, "Leave him alone'. He then turned to Hurqus and said gently,

> "Then who can be called just if I am not just". [104]

'Umar ibn Khattab himself strongly objected to the Prophet with regards to the unequal terms of the treaty of Hudaybiyyah concluded by the Prophet with the tribe of the Quraysh. The blessed Prophet did not get upset with him, but convinced him with a convincing argument.[105]

In yet another instance, a man demanded his debts from the Prophet in such a rude manner that the companions of the Prophet intended to harm him, but the Prophet said,

> "Leave him, for he [the creditor] has the right to demand it. Buy a camel of the same age and give it to him."

They said, "The camel that is available is older than the camel he demands," to which the Prophet replied,

> "Buy it and give it to him, for the best among you are those who repay their debts in the most handsome manner".[106]

The blessed Prophet imbued the values of justice and mercy together. In this way, he taught the rulers of the world how to rule so that they might know that their rank and status in human societies is like that of a kind father not like that of an absolute master and that they should always consider the best interests of their subjects instead of imposing their own whims and wishes upon them. He said,

> "I am more considerate and compassionate of the best interests of the believers than they are themselves".

He also said,

> "The Qur'an describes my rank and status in these words: *'The Prophet is closer to the believers than their own selves.'* (33:6)[107] So, if a true believer dies and leaves behind some property, his inheritance will be given to his inheritors [from the father's side], and if he leaves behind some debt to

be paid or destitute children, then I am their guardian."[108]

News and experiences of the noble character and high moral qualities of the blessed Prophet spread so widely within a short period of time and became so deeply-rooted in the hearts of the earliest Muslims that they transformed everything into the best form possible. Through them, the Prophet was able to change Arab pride into humility, mercilessness into compassion, disunity into unity, infidelity into faith, idolatry into monotheism, division into solidarity, immorality into chastity, vengefulness into forgiveness, idleness into activity, selfishness into altruism, roughness into tenderness, niggardliness into selflessness, and stupidity into sagacity and intelligence.

A summary of the Prophet's conduct and practice has been given, as far as was possible, in this article. It should be known that the Prophet's way of life is the very perfect and practical interpretation of God's heavenly Book, the Glorious Quran, which he embodied in all of the various stages of his life.

1. *al-Sirah al-Halabiyyah*, Ali ibn Burhan al-Din al-Halabi, vol. 1, p. 93
2. ibid., vol. 1, p. 95
3. ibid., vol. 1, p. 125
4. *al-Sirah al-Nabawiyyah*, Zaini Dahlan, vol.1, p. 29
5. *al-Sirah al-Halabiyyah*, vol. 1, p. 129
6. ibid. vol.1, p. 59
7. *Sahih al-Muslim*, Abul Husayn Muslim ibn al-Hallaj al-Qushayri al-Nisaburi, vol. 8, p. 222
8. *al-Sirah al-Halabiyyah*, vol. 1, p. 134
9. *I'lam al-wara'*, al-Tabarsi, p. 23
10. *Ruh al-Islam*, Sayyid Ameer Ali, p. 19
11. *al-Sirah al-Nabawiyyah*, Zaini Dahlan, vol. 1, p. 80
12. *Imta' al-Asma'*, Maqrirzi, vol.1, p. 8
13. *al-Sirah al-Halabiyyah*, vol.1, p. 111
14. *Bihar al-Anwar*, Allamah Muhammad Baqir al-Majlisi, vol. 9
15. *al-Sirah al-Halabiyyah*, vol. 1, p. 111 and *Bihar al-Anwar*, vol. 9, Bab fi Makarim al-akhlaqihi
16. *Sahih al-Bukhari*, Muhammad al-Bukhari, vol. 8, p. 79
17. *Wasa'il al-Shia'a*, Muhammad ibn Hasan al-Hurr al-Amili, Bab al-Tijarah
18. *Sahih al-Bukhari*, Muhammad ibn Isma'il al-Bukhari, vol. 2, p. 57
19. *al-Sirah al-Halabiyyah*, vol. 1, p. 150
20. ibid., p. 150
21. ibid., p. 162
22. ibid., 172
23. *Sahih al-Bukhari*, vol. 4, p. 6
24. *al-Sirah al-Halabiyyah*, vol.1, p. 157
25. ibid., vol. 1, p. 156 and *al-Sirah al-Nabawiyyah*, Zaini Dahlan, vol. 1, p. 101
26. *Sahih al-Bukhari*, vol. 2, p. 128

27. *al-Islam Ruh al-Madaniyyah*, Shaykh Mustafa al-Ghalayini, p. 182

28. *al-Sirah al-Halabiyyah*, vol. 1, 163

29. *Sahih al-Bukhari*, vol. 4, 34

30. Chapter 66 (al-Tahrim: the Prohibition), 3-5

31. *Sahih al-Muslim*, Abul Husayn Muslim ibn al-Hajjaj Qushayri al-Nisaburi, vol. 4, p. 187

32. Chapter 33 (al-Ahzab: the Allies), 28-29

33. *Sahih al-Bukhari*, vol. 7, p. 26

34. *Sahih al-Muslim*, vol. 4, p. 178

35. *Wasa'il al-Shi'ah*, Bab al-'afw 'an al-Zaujah

36. Nur al-Absar, Muhammad ibn Mu'min al-Shablanji, p. 27

37. *Sahhih al-Muslim*, vol.7, p. 77

38. *Nur al-Absar*, p. 28

39. *Sahih al-Muslim*, vol. 73

40. *Wasa'i al-Shia'ah*, Bab al-'afw 'an al-Zaujah

41. *Man la-Yahzaruh al-Faqih*, Shaykh al-Saduq Muhammad ibn Babuyah al-Qummi, p. 575

42. ibid., p. 354

43. *Sahih al-Bukhari*, vol. 3, p. 149

44. *Sahih al-Muslim*, vol. 7, p. 48

45. The content of this chapter is found in all the books of Sirah and Hadith.

46. *Sahih al-Muslim*, vol. 1, p. 163

47. ibid., vol. 7, p. 4

48. *Imta' al-Asma'*, Ahmad ibn Ali al-Maqrizi, vol. 1, p. 425

49. *Sahih al-Bukhari*, vol. 4, p. 100

50. *Sahih al-Muslim*, vol. 7, p. 14

51. *Imta' al-Asma'*, Ahmad ibn Ali al-Maqrizi, vol. 1, p. 496

52. ibid., vol. 1, p. 479

53. *Sahih al-Bukhari*, vol. 5, p. 152

54. *Bihar al-Anwar*, Bab fi Wafat al-Nabi

55. *al-Sirah al-Nabawiyyah*, Zaini Dahlan, p. 95

56. *al-Sirah al-Halabiyyah*, vol. 1, 270

57. *Sahih al-Muslim*, vol.1, p. 97

58. *Sahih al-Bukhari*, vol. 2, p. 50 and *Sahih al-Muslim*, vol. 8, p. 141

59. *Sahih al-Bukhari*, vol. 2, p. 50

60. ibid., vol. 3, p. 48

61. *Sahih al-Muslim*, vol. 3, pp. 161 and 162

62. ibid., vol. 3, p. 144

63. *Sahih al-Bukhari*, vol. 7, p. 62

64. *Sahih al-Muslim*, vol. 3, p. 82

65. ibid., 3, p. 163

66. ibid., vol. 3, p. 144

67. *Sahih al-Bukhari*, vol. 1, p. 139

68. *Sahih al-Muslim*, vol. 2, p. 42

69. *Sahih al-Bukhari*, vol. 4, p. 57

70. *Nur al-Absar*, vl. 26, p. 26 and *Bihar al-Anwar*, Bab fi Makarim Akhlaq al-Nabi

71. *Sahih al-Muslim*, vol. 6, p. 145

72. ibid., vol. 8, p. 217

73. *Bihar al-Anwar*, Bab fi Makarim Akhlaq al-Nabi

74. *Sahih al-Muslim*, vol. 8, p. 218

75. *Sahih al-Bukhari*, vol. 4, p. 190

76. *Nur al-Absar*, p. 27

77. *Sahih al-Bukhari*, vol. 8, p. 14

78. *Imta' al-Asma'*, Maqrirzi, vol. 1, p. 25

79. ibid., vol. 1, p. 472

80. *Wasa'il al-Shia'a*, Bab al-Tijarah

81. Chapter 4 (al-Nisa': Women), 5

82. Chapter 25 (al-Furqan: the Criterion), 1

83. *Imta' al-Asma'*, Maqrirzi, vol. 1, p. 18

84. *al-Sirah al-Halabiyyah*, vol. 1, pp. 334-337

85. *Sahih al-Bukhari*, vol. 5, pp. 45 and 46

86. *Sirah by Ibn Hisham*, vol. 1, p. 388

87. ibid., vol. 1, p. 275

88. *Imta' al-Asma'*, Maqrirzi, vol 1, p. 18

89. *al-Sirah al-Halabiyyah*, vol. 1, pp. 334-337

90. *Sahih al-Bukhari*, vol. 5, pp. 45 and 46

91. *Sahih al-Muslim*, vol. 8, p. 24

92. *Sirah by Ibn Hisham*, vol. 1, p. 284

93. ibid., vol. 1, p. 278

94. Chapter 5 (al-Ma'idah: the Table), 44

95. *Sahih al-Muslim*, vol. 8, p. 10

96. *Sirah by Ibn Hisham*, vol. 2, p. 253

97. *Imta' al-Asma'*, Maqrirzi, vol. 1, pp. 74, 78 and 97

98. *Sirah Ibn Hisham*, vol. 3, p. 7

99. *Imta' al-Asma', Maqrirzi, vol. 1, p. 220*

100. *Ibid. , p. 463*

101. It has to be noted that all Muslims believe in the infallibility of the Prophet with respect to his mission, but with respect to his personal life before or after the mission there are differences among different schools of Islam. Shi'a Muslims believe in the infallibility of the Prophet both before and after his mission in his delivery of the message as well as his personal life. Sunni Muslims are divided in this matter. Basically they agree on the infallibility in the delivery of message, but with respect to his personal life some believe in the possibility of committing unintentional sins and others in possibility of committing minor sins. With respect to the period before the mission started they normally do not believe in the necessity of infallibility. For further explanation see Shomali, M.A., Shi'i Islam: Origins, faith & Practices (2001), pp. 97-106(editor).

102. *Sahih al-Muslim, vol. 6, p. 16*

103. *Imta' al-Asma', Maqrirzi, vol. 1, 431*

104. *Sahih al-Bukhari, vol. 4, p. 200*

105. *Imta' al-Asma', Maqrirzi, vol. 1, p. 296*

106. *Sahih al-Bukhari, vol. 3, p. 116*

107. *Chapter 33: 6*

108. *Sahih al-Bukhari, vol. 3, 118*

The Prophet Muhammad as Portrayed in *Nahj al-Balaghah*

Mohammad Javad Shomali

One of the most reliable and authentic sources for discovering and understanding the personality of the Prophet Muhammad is to refer to his household, who were in constant relation with him and the closest to him. In this paper, the way Imam Ali has portrayed the Prophet will be studied. Imam Ali was the cousin and son-in-law of the Prophet who was brought up by the Prophet in his own house when he was a child and as a teenager, he was the first man to embrace Islam. As a young man, Imam Ali was the most faithful and bravest soldier of Islam.

I. Perfect Example and Role Model

On the subject of the Prophet being perfect example, Imam Ali says:

> "Certainly, in the Prophet of Allah (peace and blessing of Allah be upon him and his progeny) was sufficient example for you and a proof concerning the vices of the world, its defects, the multitude of its disgraces and its evil." (Sermon 160:14-159)[1]

> "You should follow your Prophet, the pure, the chaste, may Allah bless him and his descendants. In him is the example for the follower, and the consolation for the seeker of consolation. The most beloved person before Allah is he who follows His Prophet and who treads in his footsteps." (Sermon160:23-159)

II. Necessity of Following the Prophet

On the necessity of following the Prophet and his Sunnah, Imam Ali says:

> "Tread the course of the Prophet for it is the most distinguished course. Follow the *sunnah* of the Prophet for it is the most right of all behaviours." (Sermon 110:5-109)

> "He left among us the standard of right. Whoever goes further from it goes out of Faith; whoever lags behind it is ruined. Whoever sticks to it will join (the right)." (Sermon 100:2-99)

> "If we love what Allah and His Prophet hate, and hold great what Allah and His prophet hold small, that would be enough isolation from Allah and transgression of His commands." (Sermon 160:25-159)

> "Therefore, one should follow His Prophet, tread in his footsteps and enter through his entrance. Otherwise he will not be safe from ruin. Certainly, Allah made Mohammad (the peace and blessing of Allah be upon him and his descendants) a sign for the Day of Judgement; a conveyor of tidings for

> Paradise and a warner of retribution." (Sermon 160:23-159)

> "How great is Allah's blessing in that He blessed us with the Prophet as a predecessor whom we follow and a leader behind whom we tread." (Sermon 160:23-159)

> "Those companions of Muhammad (the peace and blessing of Allah be upon him and his descendants) who were the custodians (of divine messages) know that I never disobeyed Allah or His Messenger (the peace and blessing of Allah be upon him and his descendants) at all, and by virtue of the courage with which Allah honoured me I supported him with my life on occasions when even the brave turned away and the feet [of people] remained behind (instead of proceeding forward). (Sermon 197:1-196)

The Qur'an Must Be Understood with the Help of the Sunnah

As mentioned above, one of the tasks of the Prophet was to teach and explain the Qur'an. No one should think that he is able to understand the Book of God sufficiently and correctly without appealing to the teachings of the Prophet. This is especially true in cases where people who hold opposing positions, all argue from the Qur'an and try to impose their own ideas on the Qur'an. In this regard Imam Ali says:

> "Do not waste the knowledge given to you by the Holy Prophet (pbuh) and do not give up and destroy his Sunnah (traditions). Keep these two pillars of Islam (monotheism and Sunnah of the Holy Prophet (pbuh)) aloft. If you act according to my advice then you cannot be blamed for

damaging or destroying the religion." (Letter 23:1-23)

"While arguing, never quote statements from the Holy Qur'an because the passages of this Book require very careful consideration as they could be paraphrased in various ways and their meanings could be construed differently. Thus, you will adhere to your explanation and they will stick to their elucidation. Therefore, argue with them in the light of the traditions of the Holy Prophet (s) and then they will find no way to misrepresent truth." (Letter 77)

III. The World before the Advent of Islam

The era before the advent of Islam is known as the "Age of Ignorance". For a long period there were no revelations. Throughout Arabia illiteracy was so common that in Mecca only a few people were able to read and write. Superstitious beliefs and mischief was spread everywhere to the extent that people used to bury their new born daughters alive and worship their own man-made idols. For example, they used to make idols from dates and then, if there was famine, they would eat them. Inside the Ka'bah (the House of God; *Baytullah*), which was built by Abraham, the Father of all monotheistic religions, idols were kept and some people used to revolve around the Ka'bah naked. Adultery was a common phenomenon to the extent that prostitutes used to raise flags on top of their houses to attract people. Due to the lack of morality and religious belief, many people had become egotistic. They only cared about their own interests and were careless about others. People were very much divided and there were so many tribal wars that no one could dream of an enduring peace. For the purposes of survival, there was a custom of stopping wars and fights during four *haram* months. However, this was not always adhered to as people used to continue fighting even in those months by simply changing the calendar and shifting the months as they wished. In such an awkward society, not even the most optimistic people could dream of the emergence of a great religion and civilization that would change the whole world. Describing the situation before the advent of Islam, Imam Ali says:

Darkness

> "Allah deputed the Prophet when no sign of guidance existed, no beacon was giving light and no passage was clear." (Sermon 196:1-195)
>
> "I also stand witness that Muhammad is His slave and His Prophet whom He deputed when the signs of guidance were obliterated and the ways of religion were desolate." (Sermon 195:2-194)
>
> "Then, Allah, the Glorified, deputed Muhammad (the peace and blessing of Allah be upon him and his descendants) with truth, at a time when the destruction of the world was near and the next life was at hand, when its brightness was turning into gloom after shining. It had become troublesome for its inhabitants, its surface had become rough, and its decay had approached near. This was during the exhaustion of its life at the approach of signs (of its decay), the ruin of its inhabitants, the breaking of its links, the dispersal of its affairs, the decay of its signs, the divulging of its secret matters and the shortening of its length." (Sermon 198:21-197)
>
> "...till he lit fire for its seeker and lit the path for the groper in the dark. Hearts achieved guidance

through him after being ridden with troubles." (Sermon 72:2-71)

Ignorance and Mischief

"...when previously there was dark misguidance, overpowering ignorance and rude habits, and people regarded unlawful as lawful, humiliated the man of wisdom, passed lives when there were no prophets and died as unbelievers." (Sermon 151:2-150)

"Allah sent Muhammad (pbuh) as a warner (against vice) for all the worlds and a trustee of His revelation, while you people of Arabia were following the worst religion and you resided among rough stones and venomous serpents. You drank dirty water and ate filthy food. You shed the blood of each other and cared not for relationships. Idols were fixed among you and sins were clinging to you." (Sermon 26:1-26)

"Allah sent the Prophet at a time when the people were going astray in perplexity and were moving here and there in mischief. Desires had deflected them and self-conceit had swerved them. Extreme ignorance had made them foolish. They were confounded by the unsteadiness of matters and the evils of ignorance." (Sermon 95:1-94)

"Allah sent the Prophet when the mission of other Prophets had stopped and the people were in slumber for a long time. Evil was raising its head, all matters were in disruption and in the flames of war, while the world was devoid of brightness, and full of open deceitfulness. Its leaves had turned yellow and there was an absence of hope about its fruits. Water had gone underground. The minarets of guidance had disappeared and signs of destruction had appeared. It was stern to its people and frowned in the face of its seeker. Its fruit was vice and its food was carcass. Its inner dress was fear and outer cover was the sword." (Sermon 89:1-88)

Illiteracy

"Verily, Allah sent Muhammad (pbuh) when none among the Arabs read a book or claimed prophethood." (Sermon 33:1-33)

"...while no one among the Arabs read books or claimed prophethood or revelation." (Sermon 104:1-103)

Division and Discord

"The people of the earth at this time were divided into different parties, their aims were separate and their ways were diverse. They either likened Allah with His creation or twisted His Names or turned to things other than Him." (Sermon 1:41-1)

"Through him Allah united those who were divided, overpowered the powerful, overcame difficulties and levelled rugged ground, and thus removed misguidance from right and left." (Sermon 213:4-212)

IV. The Prophet Muhammad and Previous Prophecies

The advent of Prophet Mohammad was after a gap in prophesies. In addition, he was chosen by God as the Seal of the Prophets, that is, he was the final messenger of Allah on the earth and no more prophets were to follow him. Therefore, he had a very difficult mission to accomplish. He had to prepare for all the generations to come when there would be no messenger of Allah on the earth. Prophet Muhammad confirmed the previous Prophets and was prophesised by them. Previous Prophets had introduced Prophet Mohammad and his characteristics to their followers beforehand. With respect to the relation between Prophet Muhammad and previous Prophets, Imam Ali says:

Tidings about Him

> "His pledge had been taken from the Prophets, his traits of character were well reputed and his birth was honourable." (Sermon 1:41-1)

> "...till Allah deputised Muhammad (peace be upon him and his progeny) as His Prophet, in fulfilment of His promise and in completion of His Prophethood." (Sermon 1:41-1)

The Seal of the Prophethood

> "May my father and my mother shed their lives for you. O' Messenger of Allah! With your death the process of prophethood, revelation and heavenly messages has stopped, which had not stopped at the death of others (prophets)." (Sermon 235:1-233)

> "...age after age till the process came to end with our Prophet Muhammad (may Allah bless him and

his descendants) and his pleas and warnings reached finality." (Sermon 91:84, 84-90)

"My Allah, the Spreader of the surfaces (of earth) and Keeper (intact) of all skies, Creator of hearts of good and evil nature, send Thy choicest blessings and growing favours on Muhammad Thy servant and Thy Prophet who is the last of those who preceded (him) and an opener for what is closed, a proclaimer of truth with truth, a repulser of the forces of wrong and a crusher of the onslaughts of misguidance." (Sermon 72:1-71)

After an Interval from the Previous Prophets

"Allah deputised the Prophet after a gap from the previous Prophets when there was much debate (among the people)." (Sermon 133:4-132)

"Allah sent the Prophet when the mission of other Prophets had stopped and the people were in slumber for a long time." (Sermon 89:1-88)

"Allah deputed the Prophet at a time when there had been no prophets for some time. People had been in slumber for a long time and the twist of the rope had loosened." (Sermon 158:1-157)

"Allah sent him after an interval from the previous Prophets when people had fallen into errors of action and ignorance." (Sermon 94:7-93)

V. Tasks and Achievements

As the final Prophet of Allah on the earth, Prophet Mohammad had a lot of responsibilities to fulfil. He had to guide people and prepare mankind for a period with no prophets. Prophet Mohammad did his best to awaken the people and stop them from worshipping idols. He also tried hard to unite the people and mobilize their powers against ignorance, injustice and mischief. Explaining the tasks and achievements of the Prophet Muhammad, Imam Ali says:

> "He had to fight those who disobeyed him in company with those who followed him, leading them towards their salvation and hastening with them lest death overtook them. When any weary person sighed or a distressed one stopped he stood with him till he got him his aim, except the worst in whom there was no virtue at all. Eventually he showed them their goal and carried them to their places (of deliverance). Consequently, their affairs moved on and their hand-mill began to rotate (that is, their position gained strength), their spears became straight." (Sermon 104:2-103)

> "He sent him for the enforcement of His commands, for exhausting His pleas and for presenting warnings (against eternal punishment)." (Sermon 83:3-82)

> "I also stand witness that Muhammad (the peace and blessings of Allah be upon him and his progeny) is His slave and His Messenger, chosen from His creation, selected for detailing His realities, picked for His selected honour and chosen for His esteemed messages." (Sermon 178:5-177)

> "Allah sent Muhammad (pbuh) as a warner (against vice) for all the worlds and a trustee of His revelation." (Sermon 26:1-26)

"Allah deputised him (the Prophet) as a caller towards Truth and a witness over the creatures." (Sermon 116:1-115)

"Allah deputed Muhammad (pbuh) with Truth so that he may take out His people from the worship of idols towards His worship and from obeying Satan towards obeying Him and sent him with the Qur'an which He explained and made strong, in order that the people may know their Sustainer (Allah), since they were ignorant of Him, may acknowledge Him since they were denying Him, and accept Him since they were refusing (to believe in) Him." (Sermon 147:1-146)

"Allah made him responsible for conveying His message and (a means of) honour for his people, a period of bloom for the men of his days, a source of dignity for the supporters and an honour for his helpers." (Sermon 198:21-197)

"Allah guided them out of wrong and with his efforts took them out of ignorance." (Sermon 1:41)

"The Prophet lit flames for the seeker and put bright signs for the impeded." (Sermon 106:6-105)

"He sent him to manifest His commands and speak about His remembrance." (Sermon 100:2-99)

"Allah sent him with the illustrious religion, effective emblem, written Book, effulgent light, sparkling gleam and decisive injunction in order to dispel doubts, present clear proofs, administer warnings through signs and to warn of punishments." (Sermon 2:4-2)

"He called (people) to His obedience and overpowered His enemies by fighting for the sake of His religion." (Sermon 190:2-189)

"The Prophet manifested whatever he was commanded and conveyed the messages of his Lord. Consequently, Allah repaired through him the cracks, joined through him the slits and created (through him) affection among kin, although they bore intense enmity in (their) chests and deep-seated rancour in (their) hearts." (Sermon 229)

"Through him Allah united those who were divided, overpowered the powerful, overcame difficulties and levelled rugged ground, and thus removed misguidance from right and left." (Sermon 213:4-212)

"He guided the people till he took them to their (correct) position and their salvation. So their spears (that is, their officers) became straight and their conditions settled down." (Sermon 33:1-33)

"So he conveyed the message declaring the truth with it. He led the people on the (correct) highway, established signs of guidance and minarets of light, and made Islam's ropes strong and its knots firm." (Sermon 185:7-184)

"Now look at the various favours of Allah upon them, that He deputed them with a prophet who got them to pledge their obedience to him and made them unite at his call. (Look) how (Allah's) bounty spread the wings of its favours over them and made streams of blessing flow for them, and the whole community became wrapped in blissful prosperity. Consequently, they were submerged

> under its bounty and enjoyed its lush life. Their affairs were settled under the protection of a powerful ruler, and circumstances offered them overpowering honour, and all things became easy for them under the auspices of a strong country. They became rulers over the world and kings in the (various) parts of the earth. They became masters of those who were formerly their masters, and began issuing commands over those who used to command them. They were so strong that neither did their spears need testing nor did their weapons have any flaw." (Sermon 192:98-191)

VI. Noble Origin

Certainly the person who is to be chosen as the Messenger of Allah on the earth has to come from an honourable and respected family so that people do not hesitate to follow him. Prophet Muhammad was no exception. His origin was the noblest of all origins. He was of the same lineage from which Allah had brought forth all other Prophets and from which He selected His trustees. In this regard, Imam Ali says:

> "His place of stay is the best of all places and his origin is the noblest of all origins in the mines of honour and the cradles of safety. Hearts of virtuous people have inclined towards him and the reins of eyes have been turned towards him." (Sermon 96:2-95)

> "Allah deputised the Prophet with light, and accorded him the highest precedence in selection." (Sermon 213:4-212)

“His tribe is the best tribe and his lineal tree the best lineal tree whose branches are in good proportion and whose fruits are hanging (in plenty). His birth-place was Mecca, and the place of his immigration was Taybah (Medina), from where his name rose high and his voice spread far and wide.” (Sermon 161:1-160)

“I also stand witness that Muhammad is His slave, His Messenger and the Chief of His creatures. Whenever Allah divided the line of descent, He put him in the better one, and therefore, no evil-doer ever shared with him nor was any vicious person his partner.” (Sermon 214:1-213)

“Allah brought him out from the most distinguished sources of origin and the most honourable places of planting, namely from the same (lineal) tree from which He brought forth other Prophets and from which He selected His trustees. Muhammad’s descendants are the best descendants, his kinsmen the best of kin and his lineal tree the best of trees. It grew in esteem and rose in distinction. It has tall branches and unapproachable fruits.” (Sermon 94-93)

“Allah chose him from the lineal tree of prophets, from the flame of light, from the forehead of greatness, from the best part of the valley of al-Bat‘ha’, from the lamps for darkness, and from the sources of wisdom.” (Sermon 108:3-107)

VII. Characteristics

The Qur'an praises Prophet Muhammad's "noble traits of character" (68:4). Prophet Muhammad described the nature of his mission by saying, "I have been appointed to complete noble traits of character". (*Bihar al-Anwar,* Vol. 67, p. 372) In this section, we will see how Imam Ali describes the characteristics of the Prophet:

> "Then Allah deputised Muhammad as a witness, a giver of good tidings and a warner, the best in the universe as a child and the noblest as a grown man, the purest of the purified in conduct, the most generous of those who are approached for generosity." (Sermon 105:1-104)

> "Everyday he would show me, in the form of a banner, some of his high traits and command me to follow them. Every year he used to go in seclusion to the hill of Hira', where I saw him but no one else saw him." (Sermon 192:98-191)

Piety

The Prophet Mohammad was the first to exercise piety and the leader of all who fear Allah:

> "He is the foremost of all who practise piety and the power of perception of all those who achieve guidance." (Sermon 116:1-115)

> "He is the leader (Imam) of all who exercise fear (of Allah)." (Sermon 94:3-93)

Source of Mercy

The Prophet Mohammad was merciful to the extent that God says, "We have not sent you except as a mercy for all the rational inhabitants of the world" (21:107). Thus, not only was he merciful, but he was also the source of mercy and the reason for Allah's mercy on mankind. In this regard, Imam Ali says:

> "There are two things in this world that softened the Wrath of Allah and prevented its descent upon man. One has been taken away from you; hold on steadfastly to the other one. The one which has been taken away from men is the Holy Prophet and the one which is still left with them and which they must hold onto steadfastly, is repentance and atonement for sins. This is because at one place in the Holy Book Allah addressed the Holy Prophet and said He would not punish men while the Prophet was among them nor while they were asking for forgiveness (8:33)." (Wise Sayings, 88)

> "I came to know that the disturbance would not befall us so long as the Prophet (peace and blessing of Allah be upon him and his progeny) was among us. So I said, "O' Prophet of Allah, what is this disturbance of which Allah, the Sublime, has informed you?" and he replied, "O' `Ali, my people will create trouble after me."" (Sermon 156:11-155)

> "Allah repaired through him the cracks, joined through him the slits and created (through him) affection among kin although they bore intense enmity in (their) chests and deep-seated rancour in (their) hearts." (Sermon 229)

> "So he is Thy trustworthy trustee, Thy witness on the Day of Judgement, Thy deputy as a blessing and Thy messenger of truth as a mercy." (Sermon 106:6-105)

> "I stand witness that Muhammad is the choice of Allah, the conveyor of His revelation and the messenger of His mercy." (Sermon 198:2-197)

> "Through him Allah buried mutual rancour and put off the flames of revolt. Through him He gave them affection like brothers and separated those who were together (through disbelief). Through him He gave honour to the low and degraded honour (of disbelief)". (Sermon 96:2-95)

Zuhd

In many places in *Nahj al-Balaghah* Imam Ali emphasises the great danger of attachment to the materialistic world (*dunyā*). In several places, Imam refers to the Sunnah of the Prophet in this regard. The Prophet Mohammad treated this world disdainfully and regarded it lowly. He removed it from his mind, let it go away from his heart and kept it hidden from his eyes so that he should not acquire any clothing from it, or hope to stay in it. He preferred to please Allah instead of satisfying his desires. Therefore when he knew that Allah hated a thing, he hated it too; that Allah held a thing low, he held it low too; that Allah held a thing small, he held it small too. He took the least share from this world and left it hungry but entered the other world safe. Let us read some of the sayings of Imam Ali in this regard:

> "He treated this world disdainfully and regarded it lowly. He held it contemptible and hated it. He realised that Allah kept it away from him with intention and spread it out for others by way of contempt. Therefore, he remained away from it by his heart, banished its recollection from his mind and wished that its attraction should remain hidden from his eye so that he should not acquire any clothing from it, or hope for staying in it." (Sermon 109:35-108)

“Certainly, in the Prophet of Allah (peace and blessing of Allah be upon him and his progeny) is sufficient example for you and a proof concerning the vices of the world, its defects, the multitude of its disgraces and its evil, because its sides had been constrained for him, while its flanks had been spread for others; he was deprived of its milk and turned away from its adornments.” (Sermon 160:14-159)

“He took the least (share) from this world and did not take a full glance at it. Of all the people of the world he was the least satiated and the most empty of stomach. The world was offered to him but he refused to accept it. When he knew that Allah, the Glorified, hated a thing, he too hated it; that Allah held a thing lowly, he too held it lowly; that Allah held a thing small, he too held it small... The Prophet used to eat on the ground, and sit like a slave. He repaired his shoes with his own hands, and patched his clothes with his own hands. He would ride an unsaddled donkey and would seat someone behind him. If there was a curtain on his door with pictures on it he would say to one of his wives. “O’ such-and-such, take it away out of my sight because if I look at it I recall the world and its allurements.” Thus, he **removed his heart from this world** and destroyed its remembrance from his mind. He loved that its allurements should remain hidden from his eye so that he should not secure good dress from it, should not regard it a place of stay and should not hope to live in it. Consequently, he removed it from his mind, let it go away from his heart and kept it hidden from his eyes. In the same way as he who hates a thing should hate to look at it or to hear about it.” (Sermon 160:23-159)

"... he remained hungry along with his chief companions, and despite his great nearness, the allurements of the world remained remote from him." (Sermon 160:23-159)

"... He left this world hungry but entered upon the next world safe. He did not lay one stone upon another (to make a house) till he departed and responded to the call of Allah." (Sermon 160:23-159)

"Now, one should see with one's intelligence whether Allah honoured Muhammad (the peace and blessings of Allah be upon him and his descendants) as a result of this or disgraced him. If he says that Allah disgraced him, he certainly lies and perpetrates a great untruth. If he says Allah honoured him, he should know that Allah dishonoured the others when He extended the (benefits of the) world for him but held them away from him who was the nearest to Him of all men." (Sermon 160:23-159)

Calm but Quick in Responding

"He left among us the standard of right. Whoever goes further from it goes out of Faith, whoever lags behind it is ruined. Whoever sticks to it joins (the right). Its guide is short of speech, slow of steps, and quick when he rises." (Sermon 100:2-99)

Justice

"You know that the Prophet (pbuh) stoned the protected (a married) adulterer, then he also said his burial prayer and allowed his successors to inherit from him. He killed the murderer and

> allowed his successors to inherit from him. He amputated (the hand of) the thief and whipped the unprotected (unmarried) adulterer, but thereafter allowed their shares from the booty, and they married Muslim women. Thus the Prophet (pbuh) took them to ask for their sins and also abided by Allah's commands about them, but did not disallow them their rights created by Islam, nor did he remove their names from its followers." (Sermon 127:3-126)
>
> "...for his speech is just, and his judgements are clear-cut." (Sermon 72:2-71)

Bravery and Self-sacrifice

Though Prophet Mohammad was a leader and could sit baçk and just send his men to battles, he was the closest person to the enemies in battlefields and the first to fight them. Moreover, instead of trying to save the lives of his relatives by sending others to the warfront, he used to send his relatives to the front line. Thus, many of his relatives were martyred. In this regard, Imam Ali says:

> "Whenever battle became fierce, we would take refuge with the Prophet. No one was closer to the enemies than him.
>
> "While it was the practice of the Holy Prophet (pbuh) that whenever a battle was raging and his companions behaved cowardly or ran away from the battlefield (as in Badr, Uhud and Hunayn), which was usually the case, or started making the Muslims nervous (as in Khandaq), he sent members of his family (Bani Hashim) to fight out the battle to protect his companions." (Letter 9:4-9)

Moderation

> "...he threw open the truth, gave advice to the people, guided them towards righteousness and ordered them to be moderate." (Sermon 195:2-194)

Patience and Persistence

When Prophet Mohammad announced his prophethood and asked people not to worship idols, many people were united against him and tried to falsify and defeat him and his followers. The Prophet Mohammad endured all the difficulties and persisted on the truth. He did everything Allah commanded without any hesitation.

> "People's joining together to falsify him and their attempt to extinguish His light did not prevent him from it." (Sermon 190:2-189)

> "He entered every hardship in search of Allah's pleasure and endured every grief for its sake. His near relations changed themselves for him and those who were remote from him (in relationship) united against him. The Arabs let loose the reins (of their horses to quicken their march) against him, and struck the bellies of their carriers to (rouse them) in fighting against him, so much so that enemies came to his threshold from the most remote places and the most distant areas." (Sermon 194:1-193)

> "As he was burdened (with the responsibility of prophethood) so he bore it standing by Thy commands, advancing towards Thy will, without shrinking in steps of weakness of determination, listening to Thy revelation, preserving Thy testament, proceeding forward in spreading Thy commands." (Sermon 72:2-71)

"The Prophet conveyed the messages of Allah without being lazy and without any shortcoming, and he fought His enemies in the cause of Allah without being languid and without pleading excuses." (Sermon 116:1-115)

Trustworthiness

"So he is Thy trustworthy trustee, Thy witness on the Day of Judgement, Thy deputy as a blessing and Thy messenger of truth as mercy." (Sermon 106:6-105)

"He is Thy trusted trustee, the treasurer of Thy treasured knowledge, Thy witness on the Day of Judgement, Thy envoy of truth and Thy Messenger towards the people." (Sermon 72:2-71)

"So he is Thy trustworthy trustee..." (Sermon 106:6-105)

"Consequently, he fulfilled it with trustworthiness..." (Sermon 100:2-99)

Sincerity

"Then the Prophet (blessing of Allah be upon him and his descendants) did his best in giving them sincere advice, himself trod on the right path and called (them) towards wisdom and good counsel." (Sermon 95:1-94)

Giver of Tidings and Warnings

"The Prophet is the trustee of Allah's revelation, the Last of His Prophets, the giver of the tidings of His mercy and the warner of His chastisement." (Sermon 173:1-172)

> "He conveyed from Allah the pleas (against committing sins), counselled his people as a warner (against Divine chastisement) and called (people) towards Paradise as a conveyor of good tidings." (Sermon 109:35-108)

Roaming Physician

The Prophet Mohammad was a very passionate and caring guide. He could have remained in his own residence or at the mosque and waited for people to go to him. Instead, he himself used to go to people and offer them his help, healing skills and instruction. This is partly due to the nature of spiritual diseases where patients may not realize that they are ill and therefore may not seek treatment. Therefore, a physician who loves people and cares about them feels responsible to go and find those who may be in need of him. In this regard, Imam Ali says:

> "The Prophet was like a roaming physician who has set ready his ointments and heated his instruments. He uses them wherever the need arises for curing blind hearts, deaf ears, and dumb tongues. He followed the spots of negligence and places of perplexity with his medicines." (Sermon 108:3-107)

Clear and enlightening guide

Prophet Mohammad's most important task was to guide people. Therefore, Allah equipped him with undeniable proofs, clear arguments and convincing discourses. He guided people not only through his speech but also through his behaviour. Imam Ali says expands on this concept in the following ways:

> "Allah sent him with undeniable proofs, a clear success and open paths." (Sermon 185:7-184)

“His speech is clear and his silence is (indicative) like a tongue’s.” (Sermon 96-2/95)

“Allah deputised the Prophet with light, and accorded him the highest precedence in selection.” (Sermon 213:4-212)

“Allah deputed the Prophet with a sparkling light, a clear argument, an open path and a guiding book...Allah sent him with a sufficing plea, a convincing discourse and a rectifying announcement.” (Sermon 161:1-160)

“The Prophet came with (a Book containing) testimony to what (books) were already there and also with a light to be followed.” (Sermon 158:1-157)

“He is the leader (Imam) of all who exercise fear (of Allah) and a light for those who seek guidance. He is a lamp whose flame is burning, a meteor whose light is shining and a flint whose spark is bright. His conduct is upright, his behaviour is guiding, his speech is decisive and his decision is just.” (Sermon 94:3-93)

“...send Thy choicest blessings and growing favours on Muhammad Thy servant and Thy Prophet who is the last of those who preceded (him) and an opener for what is closed, a proclaimer of truth with truth, a repulser of the forces of wrong and a crusher of the onslaughts of misguidance.” (Sermon 72:2-71)

“Certainly there was in the Prophet of Allah all who **would apprise** you of the evils of this world and its defects.” (Sermon 160:23-159)

"Be it known to you, my son, that nobody has given mankind such detailed information about Allah as our Holy Prophet (pbuh). I advise you to have faith in his teachings, to make him your leader and **to accept his guidance for your salvation.**" (Letter 31:43-31)

"He introduced clear guiding signs and shining injunctions." (72:2-71)

"He left among us the standard of right." (Sermon 100:2-99)

"Through him the signs of guidance have been lighted and the gloom of blindness (misguidance) has been dispelled." (Sermon 178:5-177)

"Through him Allah disclosed the ways that had been forsaken, and destroyed the innovations that had been introduced. Through him He explained the detailed commands." (Sermon 161:1-160)

"Populated places were brightened through him when previously there was dark misguidance..." (Sermon 151:2-150)

Divinely Selected

Since Allah has knowledge about people's potential even before they are actually born, He chose the Prophet Mohammad for prophethood before his birth.

"...that Muhammad is His slave and His Prophet (peace be upon him and his progeny) and His chosen and His selected one. Muhammad's (peace be upon him and his progeny) distinction cannot be paralleled nor can his loss be made good. (Sermon 151:2-150)

> "From the time of his weaning, Allah had put a mighty angel with him to take him along the path of high character and good behaviour through day and night, while I used to follow him like a young camel following in the footprints of its mother." (Sermon 192:98-191)

VIII. Imam Ali's Attachment to the Prophet Muhammad

Not only was Imam Ali Prophet Mohammad's cousin but he was also brought up by him. The way Prophet Mohammad brought him up was very special. As Imam Ali himself says

> "He used to press me to his chest and lay me beside him in his bed, bring his body close to mine and make me smell his smell. He used to chew something and then feed me with it."

In this way Imam Ali became extremely close to Prophet Mohammad. The Prophet chose Imam Ali to be close to him because he knew Imam Ali's potential. Furthermore, Prophet Mohammad showed him his high traits and commanded him to follow them. Thus, after a while, Imam Ali reached a level at which the Prophet told him he could hear what the Prophet heard and see what the Prophet saw, though he was not a prophet. With no doubt he was the closest person to the Prophet. Imam Ali went through a very difficult time at Prophet Mohammad's death. He wanted to be with Prophet Mohammad forever. Therefore, after each time he prayed for the Prophet, he used to pray for Muslims and for himself to be with the Prophet in the hereafter.

His Upbringing by the Prophet Muhammad

Due to the fact that Prophet Mohammad knew the potential of Imam Ali (a.s.), his style of bringinghim up was very special. He treated Imam Ali better than his own children. The Prophet loved Imam Ali since his childhood. Imam Ali says:

> "Certainly, you know my position of close kinship and special relationship with the Prophet of Allah (peace and blessing of Allah be upon him and his descendants). When I was only a child he took charge of me. He used to press me to his chest and lay me beside him in his bed, bring his body close to mine and make me smell his smell. He used to chew something and then feed me with it. He found no lie in my speech, nor weakness in any act."
>
> "From the time of his weaning, Allah had put a mighty angel with him to take him along the path of high character and good behaviour through day and night, while I used to follow him like a young camel following in the footprints of its mother. Everyday he would show me, in the form of a banner, some of his high traits and commanded me to follow them. Every year he used to go into seclusion to the hill of Hira', where I saw him but no one else saw him. In those days Islam did not exist in any house except that of the Prophet of Allah (peace and blessing of Allah be upon him and his descendants) and Khadíjah, while I was the third after these two. I used to see and watch the effulgence of divine revelation and message, and breathe the scent of prophethood."
>
> "When the revelation descended on the Prophet of Allah (peace and blessing of Allah be upon him and his descendants) I heard the moan of Satan. I said, 'O Prophet of Allah, what is this moan?' and he replied, 'This is Satan who has lost all hope of being worshipped. O 'Ali, you see all that I see

> and you hear all that I hear, except that you are not a prophet, but you are a vicegerent and you are surely on (the path of) virtue.' " (Sermon 192:98-191)

His Grief for the Demise of the Prophet

The loss of Prophet Mohammad was very difficult for all Muslims. However for Imam Ali (a.s.), it was much more difficult than it was for others, as he knew the true value of Prophet Mohammad better than anyone else and was the closest person to him. Imam Ali could not endure separation from the Prophet. Therefore, each time he prayed for Prophet Mohammad, he also used to pray for all the Muslims and himself to be with the Prophet in the hereafter.

> "May my father and my mother shed their lives for you, O' Messenger of Allah! With your death the process of prophethood, revelation and heavenly messages has stopped, which had not stopped at the death of others (prophets). Your position with us (members of your family) is so special that grieving for you has become a source of consolation (to us) from all other grief; your grief is also common, so that all Muslims share it equally. If you had not ordered endurance and prevented us from bewailing, we would have produced a store of tears and even then the pain would not have subsided, and this grief would not have ended, and there would have been too little of our grief for you." (Sermon 235:1-233)

> "Then Allah chose for Muhammad, (peace be upon him and on his progeny) to meet Him, selected him for His own nearness, regarded him too dignified to remain in this world and decided to remove him from this place of trial. So He drew

him towards Himself with honour." (Sermon 94:3-93)

"I stand witness that Muhammad is His slave and His Prophet (peace be upon him and his progeny) and His chosen and His selected one. Muhammad's distinction cannot be paralleled nor can his loss be made good." (Sermon 151:2-150)

"Certainly, endurance is good except about you (your loss); fretting is bad except over you; and the affliction about you is great while every other affliction before or after it is small." (Wise Sayings, No. 292)[2]

"When the Prophet (the peace and blessing of Allah be upon him and his descendants) died, his head was on my chest, and his (last) breath blew over my palms and I passed it over my face. I performed his (funeral) ablution (may Allah bless him and his descendants), and the angels helped me. The house and the courtyard were full of them. One party of them was descending and the other was ascending. My ears continually caught their humming voices, as they invoked Allah's blessing on him, till we buried him in his grave. Thus, who can have greater rights with him than I during his life or after his death? Therefore depend on your intelligence and make your intentions pure in fighting your enemy, because I swear by Him who is such that there is no God but He, that I am on the path of truth and that they (the enemy) are on the misleading path of wrong. You hear what I say; and I seek Allah's forgiveness for myself and for you." (Sermon 197:3-196)

Wishing to be with the Prophet in the Hereafter

As mentioned above, Imam Ali was so close to Prophet Mohammad that he regarded being with the Prophet Mohammad as one of the best rewards from Allah in the hereafter.

> "...and bring us out (on the Day of Judgement) among his party." (Sermon 106:6-105)

---

[1] Since there are slight differences in numbering in different editions of *Nahj al-Balaghah,* in brackets two numberings are observed.

[2] Imam Ali said this on the grave of the Prophet Muhammad at the time of burial.

The Prophet Muhammad from the Shi'a Perspective

Muhammad Legenhausen

Introduction

> "Praise be to He who created all things; and created the best of His creations and His designs and the most refined of His prophets, Muḥammad, (may Allah bestow His blessings and benedictions upon him and on his progeny), who He refined in the best way, and whose qualities and characteristics He purified, and made him His purified one and His beloved one and gave him precedence over all of those for whom He willed purification, and prompted him according to the characteristics by which He shaped him over all those He willed to be beloved by Him."[1]

This prayer by Muḥsin Fayḍ Kāshānī (d. 1680) gives some indication of the high regard in which the Shi'a hold the Prophet Muḥammad (pbuh).[2] Indeed, he is held to be as perfect as it is possible for a human being to be; and yet, he is not considered an incarnation of divinity, for this is considered inconsistent with the greatness of God.

This paper will not review the biography of the Prophet (pbuh). That has been done in an excellent way by several others. Instead, the paper will review the role that the Prophet (pbuh) holds among Muslims, in particular among the Shi'a. The account does not aim to be historical either. It will suffice to say that Muḥammad Abu al-Qasim was born to Abdullah and Amina in 571 C.E. His mission as a prophet began when he was forty years old, and he passed away when he was sixty-three. In what follows, the image of the Prophet as it is reflected in various aspects of Shi'i thought, including the interpretation of the Qur'an (*tafsīr*), theology (*kalām*), philosophy (*ḥikmat*), and mysticism (*'irfān*) will be examined. First, however, we should recall what it means to be a prophet.

Two words are used for the special people sent by God through His mercy: *rasūl* (apostle) and *nabī* (prophet). The latter term is generally taken to include the former, that is, every apostle is a prophet but not every prophet is an apostle. The apostles are sent to bring divine law to the people. Prophets guard the law and, like the apostles, are also recipients of special revelations. The number of prophets that God has sent is said to be 124,000. The prophets are confirmed in their mission through miracles. The first prophet is said to have been Adam, and he, along with Noah, Moses, Jesus, and Muḥammad (pbuh) are considered the greatest of God's apostles. The last and most noble of all the prophets is the Apostle Muhammad (pbuh) to whom the Qur'an was revealed. The Qur'an itself constitutes the great miracle by which the prophethood of Muḥammad (pbuh) is confirmed.

Every prophet has a trustee (*waṣī*) who is charged with protecting the mission brought by the prophet. The trustee of Moses was Aaron; the trustee of Jesus was Peter; and the trustee of Muḥammad (pbuh) is 'Ali, the first of the Imams of the Shi'a.

Humanity has been entrusted by God with stewardship over the earth; so man is said to be the successor (*khalīfah*) of God on earth. Man is given this distinction over all other creatures because of the knowledge God has given him "of the names."[3] Human beings, however, betray the trust by acting unjustly, putting things out of order, and treating the trust as though it were personal property to waste and corrupt. God sends the prophets to show people how to return to their task of stewardship. The prophets are sent with good news and a warning: God is merciful and forgiving to those who will follow the way He shows them through His prophets, and there is a punishment for those who reject His guidance and mercy.[4]

So, to be a prophet is to be one of the special people that God has sent and to whom He has given revelation. But the prophets are not only vehicles for the divine message. In order to serve in this function they must be completely trustworthy, and so they are protected by God from error (*ma'ṣūm*). The Prophet Muḥammad (pbuh) is called the "seal of the prophets" in the sense that the cycle of prophethood ends with him and is sealed with the most noble of all the prophets. For the Shi'a, however, the mission of the Prophet continues through the work of the Imams.

I. The Prophet Muhammad (pbuh) in the Noble Qur'an

It is traditional to begin a discussion of just about any religious topic by examining relevant verses (*āyāt*, lit. signs) of the Qur'an, followed by narrations pertaining to the topic. For Muslims, the Qur'an is the direct revelation of God and as such, its authority supersedes all other documentation. It therefore follows that a discussion about what the Qur'an says regarding the Prophet (pbuh) should ensue. The verses of the Glorious Qur'an pertaining to Muḥammad (pbuh) and his mission, however, are too numerous to list in an article, so a selection will be given. In a sense, however, the entire Qur'an is about Muḥammad (pbuh), because it is the direct address of God to His prophet. In fact, God often addresses the Prophet directly, using the second person, as in the verse below:

> "O Prophet! Indeed We have sent you as a witness, as a bearer of good news and as a warner and as a summoner to Allah by His permission, and as a radiant lamp. Announce to the faithful the good news that there will be for them a great grace from Allah." (33:45-47)

> "Indeed We have sent you with the truth, as a bearer of good news and as a warner, and you will not be questioned concerning the inmates of hell." (2:119)

The point that the Prophet is not responsible for the deeds of others is a frequently mentioned theme.

> "Obey Allah and obey the Apostle; but if you turn away, then Our Apostle's duty is only to communicate in clear terms." (64:12)

Sometimes the Qur'an addresses the people directly and informs them about the divine mission of the Prophet Muḥammad (pbuh):

> "Muḥammad is not the father of any man among you, but he is the Apostle of Allah and the Seal of the Prophets, and Allah has knowledge of all things." (33:40)

> "As We sent to you an Apostle from among yourselves, who recites to you Our signs, and purifies you, and teaches you the Book and wisdom, and teaches you what you did not know. Remember Me, and I will remember you, and thank Me, and do not be ungrateful to Me." (2:151-152)

The Apostle of God is given authority over the people, which he is ordered to announce to them so that the people know they should follow him, and that he is responsible for guiding them.

> "Say: 'If you love Allah, then follow me; Allah will love you and forgive you your sins, and Allah is all-forgiving, all-merciful.' Say, 'Obey Allah and the Apostle.' But if they turn away, indeed Allah does not like the faithless." (3:31-32)

The following verse contains the direct address of God to Muḥammad (pbuh), and also indicates the requirement of obedience.

> "We did not send any apostle but to be obeyed, by Allah's leave. Had they, when they wronged themselves, came to you [Muḥammad] and pleaded to Allah for forgiveness, and the Apostle had pleaded for forgiveness for them, they would have surely found Allah all-clement, all-merciful." (4:64)

Although the Prophet Muḥammad (pbuh) may pray for the forgiveness of others, he does not redeem anyone's sins, and it is God who forgives. The guidance brought to humanity through the Prophet Muḥammad (pbuh) is a divine light.

> "O you who have faith! Be wary of Allah and have faith in His Apostle. He will grant you a double share of His mercy and give you a light to walk by, and forgive you, and Allah is all-forgiving, all-merciful." (58:28)

> "...O you who possess intellect and have faith! Allah has certainly sent down to you a reminder, an apostle reciting to you the manifest signs of Allah that He may bring out those who have faith

and do righteous deeds from darkness into light…" (65:10-11)

"O People of the Book! Certainly Our Apostle has come to you, clarifying for you much of what you used to hide of the Book, and pardoning much. Certainly there has come to you a light from Allah and a manifest Book. With it Allah guides those who follow His pleasure to the ways of peace, and brings them out from darkness into light by His will, and guides them to a straight path." (5:15-16)

"…[This is] a book We have sent down to you [Muḥammad (pbuh)] that you may bring mankind out from darkness into light by the command of their Lord…" (14:1)

The humble background and humanity of the Prophet Muḥammad (pbuh) is also emphasized in the Qur'an.

"It is He who sent to the unlettered an apostle from among themselves, to recite to them His signs, to purify them, and to teach them the Book and wisdom, and earlier they had indeed been in manifest error." (62:2)

In the following verse, which occurs in a longer section in which God addresses Moses, the coming of the Prophet Muḥammad (pbuh) is predicted, his humble origins are mentioned, and he is said to be sent down with a light.

"…Soon I shall appoint it [My mercy] for those who are God-wary and give the zakat and those who believe in Our signs—those who follow the Apostle, the uninstructed prophet, whose mention they find written with them in the Torah and the Gospel, who bids them to do what is right and forbids them from what is wrong, makes lawful to

> them all the good things and forbids them all vicious things, and relieves them of their burdens and the shackles that were upon them—those who believe in him, honor him, and help him and follow the light that has been sent down with him, they are the felicitous." (7:157)

In the next verse, the Prophet is commanded to announce his mission.

> "Say, 'O people! I am the Apostle of Allah to you all, [of Him] to whom belongs the kingdom of the heavens and the earth; there is no god but He; He gives life and brings death.' So have faith in Allah and His Apostle, the uninstructed prophet, who has faith in Allah and His words, and follow him so that you may be guided." (7:158)

Of special importance for the Shi'a, is the following verse, in which the importance of love for the *Ahl al-Bayt* (the family of the Prophet, literally *folk of the house*) is emphasized. In this and various other verses it is also stated that the Prophet did not want any material compensation from those he guided. The material wealth he collected was used for the needs of the community; and likewise the love he requested from the believers for his kin was also for the benefit of the community.

> "...Say, 'I do not ask of you any reward for it [bringing the divine good news] except the love of my family.'..." (42:23)

Muḥammad (pbuh) is the seal of the prophets who confirms what has come before and perfects it. Like Jesus (pbuh), he is a warner and a bringer of the good tidings of the kingdom of God:

> "...He forgives whoever He wishes, and punishes whoever He wishes, and to Allah belongs the kingdom of the heavens and the earth, and

> whatever is between them, and towards Him is the return. O People of the Book! Certainly Our Apostle has come to you, clarifying for you, after a gap in the apostles, lest you should say, 'There did not come to us any bearer of good news nor any warner.' Certainly there has come to you a bearer of good news and a warner. And Allah has power over all things." (5:18-19)

There is a lot in common between Christian and Islamic teachings about the divine kingdom, and in both traditions there is considerable ambiguity about it. What is explicitly denied in Islam, however, in stark contrast to some Christian views, is that there is a blood sacrifice by virtue of which believers may enter the kingdom. Believers are asked to repent and to establish a just society. According to the Shi'a, this virtuous city is headed by the Imam of the Age.

II. The Prophet Muhammad (pbuh) in the Literature of Hadith

The narrations that report the deeds and sayings of the Prophet are called *ahadith* (sing., *hadith*). They are found in various collections that have been compiled by Muslims throughout the ages. Among the Sunni Muslims, there are six standard collections that contain sound reports. For the Shi'a, there are various collections of reports, and the authenticity of each narration is evaluated by scholars on the basis of the chain of transmission (*isnād*) that is recorded along with the ahadith. In addition, there are some very famous ahadith attributed to the Prophet that lack proper credentials. The lack of documentation does not imply that they are not authentic, though. The fact that they have remained in circulation is itself a testimony to their influence in the Muslim community. Many of these unauthenticated narrations are common to the Shi'i and the Sunni communities.

Another important difference between Sunni and Shi'i collections of narrations, is that the Shi'i collections include reports of the words and deeds of all of the fourteen infallibles, the Prophet, his daughter Fāṭimah, and the twelve Imams. The Shi'a justify the inclusion of these narrations on the grounds that all fourteen personalities provide sources for the sunnah of the Prophet, since all of them are completely imbued with his character and teachings.

The subject matter of the ahadith varies widely, and includes matters of worship, trade, spirituality, politics, morals, health, etiquette, theology and law, to name a few. The importance of the ahadith to the religious practice of Muslims may be understood by reflecting on the fact that instructions for the ritual prayers are not found in the Qur'an. On the basis of the Qur'an alone, without the literature of hadith, scholars would not be able to authenticate many of the most important rituals and precepts of Islam.

In order to understand the Prophet (pbuh) on the basis of the Shi'i literature of hadith, the important collections should be reviewed. This will aid the discovery of how the Prophet described himself and his mission, and how the other infallibles described him and his mission. In this paper, it is only possible to suggest this task as a research option, and offer a couple of ahadith by way of samples.

One of the most famous ahadith in which the Prophet describes his mission is as follows:

> "Verily, I have been commissioned to complete the perfection of morals."[5]

Another frequently mentioned hadith in the books of the Shi'a is:

"I am the city of wisdom, and 'Alī is its gate."[6]

One should recall that wisdom is one of the four cardinal virtues of Aristotle; so, it is natural that one who is commissioned to complete the perfection of morals should be the city of wisdom.

In addition to the words of wisdom that can be found in the literature of hadith about moral advice, spiritual insight, and legal rulings, there are several outstanding events in the life of the Prophet (pbuh) that are also reported in this literature and that should be mentioned. For example, there is the final victory over the pagans in Mecca, when the Prophet (pbuh) forgave his sworn enemies, or the event of Ghadīr, when the Prophet (pbuh) took the hand of 'Alī and told the assembled crowd that whoever accepted his (Muḥammad (pbuh)'s) guardianship should accept 'Alī (a.s.)'s guardianship after him; to mention just two of the many fateful events. Another event that is of particular importance is the *mi'rāj* or "Night Journey", about which there are several verses in the Qur'an[7] and a number of reports.[8] The mi'rāj has been subject to numerous commentaries and interpretations of various sorts. The Prophet (pbuh) himself is said to have remarked,

"The prayer (*ṣalāh*) is the mi'rāj of the believer."

> In brief, the angel Gabriel woke Prophet Muhammad (pbuh) and instructed him to mount Burāq (usually depicted as a winged horse with a human face), on which he flew to the Temple at Jerusalem where all the previous prophets had assembled and prayed behind him. He was then guided by Gabriel to the seven heavens, in each of which he met a prophet. After this they visited hell and paradise. When they reached the upper bounds of paradise, Gabriel admitted that he could advance no further, but urged Prophet Muhammad (pbuh) to go on. Prophet Muhammad (pbuh)

> entered into a pure light, received instructions for his followers, and then returned, met Gabriel, and descended, saying farewell to the various prophets on the way down.

Fayḍ Kāshānī finishes his collection of narrations about the *mi'rāj* with the following, in which the Prophet is reported to have answered as below to a question about the voice of God during the *mi'rāj*:

> "My Lord spoke to me with the voice of 'Alī ibn Abī Ṭālib and said, 'O Ahmad! I am an Entity that is not like anything else. I cannot be compared to anything else and I know all the secrets of your heart. With the exception of 'Alī ibn Abī Ṭālib, you have no other close friend. Thus, I speak to you with the voice of 'Alī ibn Abī Ṭālib so that your heart will be at ease."

One of the frequently cited collections of narrations attributed to Imam 'Alī is *Nahj al-Bālaghah*.[9] In this work there are many narrations in which Imam 'Alī describes the Prophet (pbuh). Below are a few of the most representative passages quoted from his sermons.

In this sermon, Imam 'Alī instructs his followers about how to invoke blessings on the Prophet (pbuh):

> "My Allah, the Spreader of the surfaces (of the earth) and the Keeper (intact) of all the skies, Creator of hearts on good and evil nature, send Thy choicest blessings and growing favors on Muhammad Thy servant and Thy Prophet who is the last of those who preceded (him) and an opener for what is closed, a proclaimer of truth with truth, a repulser of the forces of wrong and a crusher of the onslaughts of misguidance. As he

was burdened (with the responsibility of prophethood), so he bore it, standing by Thy commands, advancing towards Thy will, without shrinking from steps of weakness of determination, listening to Thy revelation, preserving Thy testament, proceeding forward in the spreading of Thy commands till he lit fire for its seeker and lighted the path for the groper in the dark.

"Hearts achieved guidance through him after being ridden with troubles. He introduced clearly guiding signs and shining injunctions. He is Thy trusted trustee, the treasurer of Thy treasured knowledge, Thy witness on the Day of Judgment, Thy envoy of truth and Thy Messenger towards the people. My Allah prepare a large place for him under Thy shade and award him multiplying good, by Thy bounty.

"My Allah, give height to his construction above all other constructions, heighten his position with Thee, grant perfection to his effulgence and perfect for him his light. In reward for his discharging Thy prophethood, grant him that his testimony be admitted and his speech be liked for his speech is just, and his judgments are clear-cut. My Allah put us and him together in the pleasures of life, continuance of bounty, satisfaction of desires, enjoyment of pleasures, ease of living, peace of mind and gifts of honor." (Sermon 70/72: 146).

In a number of places, Imam 'Alī explains how the people had gone astray and were guided by the Prophet (pbuh), such as in the following instance:

> "Allah sent the Prophet at a time when the people were going astray in perplexity and were moving here and there in mischief. Desires had deflected them and self-conceit had swerved them. Extreme ignorance had made them foolish. They were confounded by the unsteadiness of matters and the evils of ignorance. Then the Prophet (blessing of Allah be upon him and his descendants) did his best in giving them sincere advice, himself trod on the right path and called (them) towards wisdom and good counsel." (Sermon 93/95: 184).

Later Imam 'Alī extols the virtues of the Prophet (pbuh) as follows:

> "His station is the best of all stations and his origin the noblest of all origins in the mines of honor and the cradles of safety. Hearts of virtuous persons have been inclined towards him and the reins of eyes have been turned towards him. Through him Allah buried mutual rancor and put off the flames of revolt. Through him He gave them affection like brothers and separated those who were together (through disbelief). Through him He gave honor to the low and degraded the honor (of disbelief). His speech is clear and his silence is (as indicative) as a tongue's speech. (Sermon 94/96: 184-185).

Imam 'Alī prays for the Prophet (pbuh) as follows:

> "The Prophet lighted flames for the seeker and put bright signs for the impeded. So he is Thy trustworthy trustee, Thy witness on the Day of Judgment, Thy deputy as a blessing and Thy messenger of truth as mercy. My Allah distribute to him a share from Thy Justice and award him

> multiples of good by Thy bounty. My Allah heighten his construction over the constructions of others, honor him when he comes to Thee, dignify his position before Thee, give him honorable position, and award him glory and distinction, and bring us out (on the Day of Judgment) among his party, neither ashamed, nor repentant, nor deviators, nor pledge-breakers, nor those gone astray, nor misleaders, nor those seduced." (Sermon 104/106: 194).

In the following narration, Imam 'Alī compares the Prophet (pbuh) to a "roaming physician," that is, to one who brings the cure where it is needed instead of waiting for patients to come to him.

> "The Prophet was like a roaming physician who has set ready his ointments and heated his instruments. He uses them wherever the need arises for curing blind hearts, deaf ears, and dumb tongues. He followed with his medicines the spots of negligence and places of perplexity." (Sermon 106/108: 195)

Imam 'Alī cites the humility and other virtues of the Prophet (pbuh) as he encourages the people to follow him:

> "You should follow your Prophet, the pure, the chaste, may Allah bless him and his descendants. In him is the example for the follower, and the consolation for the seeker of consolation. The most beloved person before Allah is he who follows His Prophet and who treads in his footsteps. He took the least (share) from this world and did not take a full glance at it. Of all the people of the world he was the least satiated and the most empty of stomach. The world was offered

to him but he refused to accept it. When he knew that Allah, the Glorified, hated a thing, he too hated it; that Allah held a thing low, he too held it low; that Allah held a thing small, he too held it small. If we love what Allah and His Prophet hate and hold great what Allah and His prophet hold small that would be enough isolation from Allah and transgression of His commands.

"The Prophet used to eat on the ground, and sat like a slave. He repaired his shoes with his own hands, and patched his clothes with his own hands. He would ride an unsaddled ass and would seat someone behind him. If there was a curtain on his door with pictures on it he would say to one of his wives. "O' such-and-such, take it away out of my sight because if I look at it I recall the world and its allurements." Thus, he removed his heart from this world and destroyed its remembrance from his mind. He loved that its allurements should remain hidden from his eye so that he should not secure good dress from it, should not regard it a place of stay and should not hope to live in it. Consequently, he removed it from his mind, let it go away from his heart and kept it hidden from his eyes. In the same way that he who hates a thing should hate to look at it or to hear about it.

"Certainly there was in the Prophet of Allah all that would apprise you of the evils of this world and its defects, namely that he remained hungry along with his chief companions, and despite his great nearness the allurements of the world remained remote from him. Now, one should see with one's intelligence whether Allah honored Muhammad (the peace and blessings of Allah be upon him and his descendants) as a result of this or

> disgraced him. If he says that Allah disgraced him, he certainly lies and perpetrates a great untruth. If he says Allah honored him, he should know that Allah dishonored the others when He extended the (benefits of the) world for him but held them away from him who was the nearest to Him of all men.
>
> "Therefore, one should follow His Prophet, tread in his footsteps and enter through his entrance. Otherwise he will not be safe from ruin. Certainly, Allah made Muhammad (the peace and blessings of Allah be upon him and his descendants) a sign for the Day of Judgment, a conveyor of tidings for Paradise and a warner of retribution. He left this world hungry but entered upon the next world safe. He did not lay one stone upon another (to make a house) till he departed and responded to the call of Allah. How great is Allah's blessing in that He blessed us with the Prophet as a predecessor whom we follow and a leader behind whom we tread." (Sermon 158/160: 265-266).

In harmony with the verse of the Qur'an,

> "Hold fast, altogether, to Allah's cord, and do not be divided. And remember Allah's blessing upon you when you were enemies, then He brought your hearts together, so you became brothers with His blessing, and you were on the brink of a pit of Fire, whereat He saved you from it." (3:103),

Imam 'Alī (a.s.), in his sermons, repeatedly makes the point that the Prophet (pbuh) taught the Arabs, who were in a state of ignorance where they were killing one another, how God would replace their enmity with friendship, as in the following excerpt:

> "The Prophet manifested whatever he was commanded and conveyed the messages of his Lord. Consequently, Allah repaired through him the cracks, joined through him the slits and created (through him) affection among kin although they bore intense enmity in (their) chests and deep-seated rancor in (their) hearts." (Sermon 228/231: 381).

The picture of the Prophet (pbuh) that emerges from the Shi'ite narrations, such as those found in the *Nahj al-Balāghah* and elsewhere, is that of a divine guide destined from eternity to show humanity its potential. The honor and virtue of the Prophet Muḥammad (pbuh) is so great that it justifies the entire creation.

III. The Prophet Muhammad (pbuh) in Shi'ite Kalām

The high stature of Prophet Muḥammad (pbuh) that can be appreciated by reflection on the Qur'an and ahadith is formalized in the creedal statements of the Shi'ite theologians. The early theologians debated about the most excellent of all creatures. The Shi'a came to the conclusion that the prophets and Imams are superior to angels.[10] (There were even some extremists who claimed that ordinary Shi'ites were superior to the angels, but this idea was rejected and considered heterodox.)[11] Shaykh Ṣadūq (d. 991) writes:

> "It is necessary to believe that Allah the Mighty and Glorious did not create any created thing more excellent than Muhammad and the Imams, peace on them, that they are the most loved of creatures in the eyes of Allah, and the most noble and the foremost among them, on account of their acceptance of Him (as their Lord). When Allah took the pledge (mīthāq) of the prophets and

> "required them to bear witness of themselves (saying): Am I not your Lord? and they said: Yes, verily" (7:172).
>
> "And verily Allah sent His Prophet Muhammad (with a message) to the other prophets in the world of atoms (*adh-dharr*). And verily Allah the Mighty and Glorious gave to each prophet (that is, knowledge, power, and so on) according to the extent of his cognition (*ma'rifah*), while the cognition of our Prophet Muhammad (pbuh) was greater and more sublime, for it took precedence in accepting Allah (as the Supreme Being).
>
> "We believe that Allah, Blessed and Exalted is He above all, created the whole of creation for him (the Prophet) and for the People of his House, and that, but for them, Allah, Glory be to Him, would not have created the heavens or the earth, Paradise or Hell, Adam or Eve, the angels or (any) created thing (*shay'*)—the Blessings of Allah upon them all."[12]

In view of this status, the theologians developed a doctrine of infallibility (*'ismah*) with regard to the prophets, the daughter of the Prophet, Fatimah, the Imams, and the angels. According to this doctrine, the infallibles do not commit any sins, major or minor, and they act entirely according to the will of God. They possess attributes of perfection and knowledge from the beginning until the end of their careers.[13]

According to Shaykh Mufid (d. 1022), all of the prophets are protected by God from committing any major sin or any sin that could bring discredit to them; while Prophet Muhammad (pbuh) is absolutely protected from committing even the slightest sin that is possible for other prophets (prior to their mission).[14] Mufid exceeds Saduq in his attribution of infallibility for, while Saduq holds that it was possible for the Prophet to be negligent in his prayer in such a way as to fall short of being even a minor sin, Mufid holds that such negligence is also impossible, even if it does not constitute a sin.

For anyone who wants to understand the development of Shi'ite theology, *The Abstract of Beliefs* (*Tajrīd al-I'tiqād*) by Khwājah Naṣīr al-Dīn Ṭūsī (d. 1274) is essential. This work has become the most important statement of Shī'ī theology for its period, largely due to the commentary written by Ṭūsī's student, Jamāl al-Dīn Ḥillī (d. 1325). This work represents the integration of Islamic philosophy in Shi'ite theology.

The section on prophethood (*nubuwwah*) is relatively short: fifteen pages in the Arabic edition together with 'Allāmah Ḥillī's commentary, compared with fifty-four pages for the previous section on proofs for the existence of God, and thirty-six pages on imamate in the next section. The section on prophethood is divided into discussions of seven problems: (1) the excellence of the prophetic mission; (2) the necessity for the prophetic mission; (3) the necessity for infallibility; (4) the way of knowing the truth of the prophet; (5) miracles; (6) the necessity of the prophetic mission at all times; (7) the prophethood of our Prophet, Muḥammad (pbuh), may divine blessings be with him and his family.

It is the seventh section that is most pertinent to our concerns here. It is affirmed that the Prophet Muḥammad (pbuh) is indeed a true prophet and evidence is found for this in his miracles, (most prominently the Qur'an), and in his great sincerity and trustworthiness, combined with his claim to being a prophet. Various narrations in addition to verses of the Qur'an are brought to support the claim of the universality of the prophetic mission, against those who viewed it as limited to the Arabs. Finally, the old discussion of the superiority of the prophet to the angels is mentioned, but a philosophical twist is given to the discussion. The reason for the superiority of the prophets to the angels is that the reasoning of the prophets must overcome their other powers, such as lust and anger, while the angels are considered to be free from such emotions. Hence, the philosophical point is made that the superiority of the prophets is consistent with the superiority of their reasoning, and this faculty is superior to what is found in the case of the angels because it must overcome the limitations, desires and other emotions characteristic of humanity.[15]

As examples of contemporary Shi'ite theology, we may consider Ayatollah Ja'far Sobhani's *Doctrines of Shi'i Islam* and Ayatollah Miṣbāḥ Yazdī's *Amūzesh-e Aqā'id* (*Theological Instructions*), both of which are written in Persian. Like the *Tajrīd* of Naṣīr al-Dīn Ṭūsī, the section on prophethood in Sobhani's book is divided into general considerations about prophethood, and specific discussions of the Prophet Muḥammad (pbuh).[16]

The specific discussions of the Prophet Muḥammad (pbuh) begin with the confirmation of his prophethood, which is provided in three ways: (1) by miracles accompanying the prophetic call; (2) by the accumulated evidence from companions and witnesses in support of the truth of the call; and (3) by verification from reports attributed to previous divine messengers. Each of these is discussed separately and is then followed by an elaboration of two distinctive features of the Prophet Muhammad (pbuh): (1) the universality of his call; and (2) his being the final prophet sent by God for mankind, whose law has jurisdiction until the end of time.

Ayatollah Miṣbāḥ's book has a section on leadership, which may be divided into chapters dealing with prophethood and those dealing with imamate. There are fifteen (short) chapters on prophethood. The first ten of these deal with problems pertaining to prophethood in general, including the traditional issues such as the need for prophets, how they can be recognized, miracles and infallibility, but also including some new discussions, such as the relationship between the prophet and the people and the opposition they found in some quarters.

The early books of doctrinal statements were designed to define orthodoxy. They tended to be spare, in order to be less exclusive. As time went on, issues were discussed in such works that were admittedly controversial, so that difference of opinion would not amount to heresy but the inclusion of such topics could facilitate the understanding of the creed. So, for example, it is necessary for Muslims to believe in prophethood, generally, and in the prophethood of Muḥammad (pbuh) specifically. This requires the understanding that prophets act as divine guides. How the prophets play this role of divine guidance is subject to disagreement, but our understanding of the issue may be increased through discussions of the relationship that the prophets had with the people they addressed. It is with a view to increase our understanding of the way the prophets function as guides that Ayatollah Misbah discusses the relationship between the prophets and the people.

Although the social dimension of prophethood does not feature in most books designed to state the Shi'ite creed, it was discussed earlier in the philosophical tradition from Fārābī and Ibn Sina to Mulla Sadra, as we shall see later.

All of the prophets faced opposition to their mission, primarily from the wealthy and powerful. This opposition was directed against the prophets themselves and against their followers. Opposition took the form of threats, insults and violence, on the one hand, and bribery and temptations, on the other. The response of the prophets to such opposition was through words and deeds. In their teachings, the prophets appealed to different classes of people through the use of rational argument, miracles, and the employment of rhetorical techniques. They also confirmed the prophets that preceded them and those (if any) to come. In their deeds, the prophets made use of supernatural powers for their defence, as with the performance of miracles, and to more natural features of character, such as charisma, the exhibition of justice and mercy and other virtues, which may be exercised through various tactics, such as jihad, emigration, the forming of alliances, concealment, and so on. In all of these a balance was displayed between firmness and tolerance.

The five chapters of *Amūzesh-e Aqā'id* on the Prophet of Islam (pbuh) begin with verification of his claim to prophethood, the miraculous nature of the Qur'an, the universality of Islam and its eternity, and the finality of the mission of the Prophet Muhammad (pbuh).[17]

IV. The Prophet Muhammad (pbuh) in Islamic Philosophy

As one might expect, given the nature of philosophy, attention to the Prophet in Islamic philosophy focuses more on his role as a prophet and less on the individual aspects of his life and character. There are narrations according to which the first thing that God created was the intellect (*'aql*); and several such narrations open the important early Shi'ite collection, *Uṣūl al-Kāfī* by Kulaynī. Given the narrations we have already mentioned to the effect that the first thing that God created was the divine light of Muḥammad (pbuh), it would be only natural to speculate about how this prophetic light could be identified with the intellect.

As is well known, Neoplatonism figures prominently among the philosophical views taken into consideration by the early Muslim philosophers. The Muslim philosophers from Kindi (d. c.866-873) onward interpreted divine creation by means of a theory of emanation in which the first things created were a series of intellects. Each of the intellects was associated with a celestial sphere or an angel or both. The schemes that were developed do not correspond exactly to what is found in the traditional collections of narrations, but common themes stand out.

The philosophers allowed for a kind of unification between the prophetic intellect and the intellect of the angel of revelation.

However, the active intellect with which the prophetic intellect became unified was not the first emanation, but the lowest (traditionally the tenth) emanation, or active intellect. According to Fārābī (c. 870-950), the human intellect is at first merely potential. When the potential intellect takes on intellectual forms, it becomes the actual intellect. When it reflects upon itself and becomes self-intelligible and self-intellective, Farabi calls it the "acquired intellect". The acquired intellect is capable of contemplating the tenth emanation, the Active Intelligence, identified with the Holy Spirit (often named as Gabriel, the angel of revelation, not to be confused with the Christian understanding of the Holy Spirit). As Fazlur Rahman explains,

> "in a few unique cases, when this happens, the Active Intelligence becomes the form of the *'aql mustafāḍ* [acquired intellect] and the perfect philosopher, or the Imam (or the Prophet) comes into existence."[18]

The theory of prophecy as expounded by Muslim philosophers is complex and remains quite controversial. There are also important developments in the history of Islamic philosophy on this issue. However, aside from such details, and without detracting from their importance, there are a couple of general points worthy of notice. First, the prophets are treated by the philosophers, not merely as people to whom a divine message is brought, but as exceptional human beings who in some way are united with immaterial divine emanations. Secondly, the idea of the prophets being essentially immaterial intellects without compromising their humanity (since these immaterial intellects are also embodied) is a theme that is common between the Shi'a and the philosophers. With the Shi'a, the philosophers, and, as we will see shortly, with the Sufis, there is an exaltation of the prophets and other divine guides. (This view can also be found among some of the Mu'tazilites.) Given the difficulties involved in the historical research on early Islam, it is beyond the author's capacity to offer a convincing case that the high status given to the divine guides in Shi'ism is causally responsible for analogous outcomes in Islamic philosophy and mysticism; however, there are a number of common themes to be found among the Shi'i theologians, the Muslim philosophers and the Sufis that distinguish their views from the Ash'arite theology that has tended to dominate Sunni Islam. Among these themes, one of the most important is the idea of the divine guide.

In addition to their works about the nature of the prophetic intellect and its (partial) union with the active intelligence, the Muslim philosophers wrote visionary recitals in which the role of the prophet is described through the use of parables. The most famous of such essays are those of Ibn Sina[19] and Sohravardi.[20]

In addition to Ibn Sina's visionary recitals, there is also an essay on the *mi'rāj* attributed to him (and taken to be authentic in the Iranian tradition. Some have raised questions about this, although it is generally agreed that there is a high probability that the author was a Shi'ite).[21] In this work, Ibn Sina expresses his characteristic intellectual idea of knowledge of the divine. Henry Corbin describes his essay as follows:

> "Two *ḥadīth* figure in it, suggesting a *ta'wīl* [interpretation] that will safely conduct our Imāmite philosophers to their goal. The Prophet, addressing the First Imām ('Center of Wisdom, Heaven of Essential Reality'), speaks as follows: 'While the common run of mankind approaches the Creator through every kind of piety, do thou approach Him by every form of intelligence: thou art before them all." And again: "O 'Alī! while men take such pains to multiply their acts of adoration, do thou attend to Knowledge of the intelligible world [*ma'qūl*], so that thou shalt be before them all.'"'[22]

As Peter Heath explains, the essay consists of two main parts: in the first part, Ibn Sina provides a summary of his psychology and epistemology by means of which he will explain the *mi'rāj*; in the second part he uses this philosophical theory to provide a running commentary and exegesis of the events reported in the hadiths about the *mi'rāj*.

Henry Corbin contrasts the "orthodox" interpretation of the *mi'rāj* as a corporeal flight into the heavens, with the philosophical interpretation of Ibn Sina of the *mi'rāj* as a mental or spiritual excursion.[23] However, Ibn Sina did not deny the physical nature of the ascent altogether, so that it did not have anything to do with mounting a marvelous steed and passing through the heavens; rather he interpreted the religious images as symbols for a deeper philosophical reality. The physical nature of the ascent is rightly accepted by the masses, but requires interpretation for the elite to be able to understand it philosophically. For those incapable of such an understanding, the marvel is not to be denied. Intellectual truths as understood in philosophy are given sensible configuration in religion, according to the Muslim philosophers, so that, for example, nothingness takes the sensible form of darkness. "In all this," Fārābī says, "the symbols should be as near to reality as possible."[24] This wording is unfortunate, for it invites the reaction of the orthodox that it implies that reality is to be found in philosophy and not in religion. There is an opposition, as Corbin notices, instead of complimentary (though hierarchically arranged) perspectives, as we will see which is suggested by Mulla Sadra.

Sohravardi does not have a commentary on the *mi'rāj*, but Corbin claims that his "A Tale of Occidental Exile" may be considered as such.[25] Aside from salutations, this essay does not explicitly mention the Prophet at all; but it describes how one can learn to escape the prison of the material or "occidental" world and ascend to join sublime celestial bodies and go beyond them to a paradise on Mt. Sinai. So, what we find in such allegories are symbolic treatments of what their authors take to be the essential mission of the prophets.

The Muslim philosophers also emphasized the social and political dimensions of prophethood. Ibn Sina held that the moral order of society backed by divine law is needed to curb the destructive results of unbound self-interest. For ordinary people, the divine law merely serves to organize society; but for those who are capable of higher motivation, the law becomes a basis for the acquisition of virtue. The law can only play this dual role of organizing society and serving as the basis for moral development if it is brought by a prophet. Only a prophet, one who has achieved some degree of union with the active intelligence, is able to understand how laws can embody the intellectual forms of practice whose realization will lead to felicity. Furthermore, it is only a prophet who can establish the religious institutions that will serve to motivate obedience to the law and serve as reminders of its real purpose even after they themselves have passed away.[26] Ibn Sina introduces his explanation of worship in this manner, and comments,

> "It should be said to people, 'these actions will bring you near to God and would cause the blessed good to come to you'—and indeed, they should be really such."[27]

In this last phrase we find, again, the idea that the esoteric is not opposed to the exoteric, but compliments it and provides its depth and goal.

Islamic philosophy among the Shi'a has continued its own path in the shadow of the towering figure of Mulla Sadra (d. 1640). He provides a discussion of prophethood in his *Al-Shawāhid al-Rubūbiyah (Witnessings of the Lord).*[28] This book is divided into five major divisions, the last of which is on prophethood and *wilāyāt.*[29] This division, in turn, is divided into two parts: the characteristics of the Prophet (pbuh); and the criteria for establishing the truth of the claim to prophethood. The first part, in turn, is divided into ten sections: (I.1) the degree of the prophets compared with the other degrees of human beings; (I.2) the principles of miracles and departures from what is normal; (I.3) three features: (I.3.a) purification of the soul, (I.3.b) ability to see the hidden world while awake through the fortified power of the imagination, and (I.3.c) other powers of the soul; (I.4) the difference between prophets, the soothsayers and others; (I.5) the qualities of prophetic warnings; (I.6) the differences among revelation, inspiration, and learning; (I.7) the quality of the unity of the prophet with the world of divine revelation, the judgment of the Lord, the reading of the protected tablet, the effaced tablet, and the denial of the abrogation of precepts; (I.8) what has come down in reports about attributions of hesitation to God; (I.9) that the prophet is situated at the boarder between the world of intellect and the sensory world; (I.10) the number of attributes that the Prophet personally must have as primary head.

The second part, (about the criteria for establishing the truth of the prophetic claim) is divided into nine sections: (II.1) proving the existence of the prophet; (II.2) what is needed and necessary in law (*sharīʿah*) for ordinary people; (II.3) the wisdom of the political arrangements and punishments; (II.4) the difference between prophethood, the sharīʿah, and politics; (II.5) an indication of the secrets of the sharīʿah and the benefits of obedience; (II.6) the advantages of certain acts of worship; (II.7) a criteria by which to distinguish major from minor sins; (II.8) the exterior and interior and the first and last of the sharīʿah; (II.9) the sense in which prophethood and the prophetic mission on earth have been discontinued.

Although it would take too long to summarize all of these sections, a brief review is provided of those sections that are most relevant to the theory of prophethood and the character of the Prophet (pbuh).

(I.1) Human beings have different degrees and stations, some of which pertain to the sensory world, some to the imagination, some to the world of thought and intellectual perceptions, and some to the world of witnessings (*shuhūd*) and their objects (*'ayān*). Just as these worlds are ranked one above the other, so too, there are degrees and rankings within each of these worlds. Even in the sensory world, for example, the station of the butterfly is higher than that of the caterpillar. The station and status of every person is in accordance with the station and status of his or her perceptions. For the angels there are also levels and stations. These worlds of different levels and the levels within them are the places through which human beings are constantly traveling, so that they can go from a beastly state to an angelic one, and from there they can ascend to the level of the lovers of God. The highest degree of human perfection is the station of the prophets and *awliyā*. (337-340/466-470)

(I.2) The people who reach the most comprehensive levels of perfection with regards to the three worlds of sensation, imagination, and intellectuality, are the vicegerents of God. Such people are deserving of leadership over other people, and so God appoints them to be his apostles, gives them revelations, by means of miracles confirms them, and provides them with divine aid against their enemies. (340-341/470-471)

(I.3.a) The first of three features of the prophets mentioned by Mulla Sadra is that God elevates the rational soul of the prophet with respect to his theoretical faculties to a purity so intense that it becomes similar to the great spirit (*rūḥ al-a'ẓam*) and is united with it, whenever he wants, without need for much meditation or thinking until knowledge of the world effuses into him without the mediation of human learning. This becomes so intense that the oil of the receptive intellect is ignited by the flame of the active intelligence, which is not outside the reality of the sacred essence.[30] (341/471)

Mulla Sadra explains that just as there are some human souls that are so weak that they have trouble learning anything, there are others who seem to guess or estimate correctly with hardly any instruction. The prophets have the most excellent powers of estimation and are united with the world of light. Their illumination reaches such an extent and their powers of judgment are such that in a short time they are able to understand things ordinary people are incapable of comprehending, except to some extent over a long period of spiritual discipline and meditation. In its most excellent parts, the performance of miracles is due to this ability. This feature is shared by both the prophets and the *awliyā*. (342/472)

(I.3.b) As for the second feature, it is that the imaginative faculty (*takhayyul*) becomes so powerful that the hidden world is witnessed while awake and it takes imaginary and occult forms. Sensible sounds are heard from the celestial kingdom (*malakūt*) from the midst of the station of the celestial earth (*hūrqaliyā*) or from other places, so that he [the prophet] sees an angel bearing the revelation; and what he hears are words configured by Allah, the Exalted, or a book or pages. In this the *awliyā* do not have a share, in contrast to the first feature. (342/472)

(I.3.c) As for the third feature, it is the faculty of the soul with respect to the practical part of it and its power of excitation that has an influence over the matter of the world. It is through this power that miracles are performed, such as when a non-living material object takes the form of a snake, or the weather changes on command, or the sick are cured. In these and other affairs bodies become obedient to the influence of souls. Mulla Sadra compares this with the physical effects that occur in the body prior to coitus that results from the form of the sexual act in the mind. Hence, it is not surprising that in those people for whom the practical part of the soul has been perfected by God, its influence extends beyond their own bodies to other bodies and other aspects of nature, just as sexual arousal occurs without physical contact. At the highest level, the most perfect soul will be able to influence what occurs in all the bodies of the entire world, in the same way that ordinary souls are able to influence the movements of their own specific bodies. (342-344/472-474)

There follows a short section called *tadhnīb 'arshī* (throne-like appendage).

> "The substance of prophethood is like a collection of lights, lights pertaining to the intellect, the soul, and to the senses. By the spirit and intellect, he becomes a seraph (*malakan min al-muqarabīn*), by the mirror of his soul and his mind, he becomes a celestial sphere far above the animal world and a tablet protected from the touch of the devils, and by his sensory faculties he becomes a king of the greatest sultans.
>
> So, the Prophet, by his unique personality, is like an angel, a celestial sphere, and a king. He is the gathering of the three realms in their perfection. By his spirit, he is of the exalted kingdom (*malakūt*); by his soul, he is of the middle kingdom, and in accordance with the lower kingdom, he is the vicegerent of Allah and the collection of the places for the manifestation of the divine names and the perfections of Allah completely, as with the saying of our Prophet (pbuh), 'There has been given to me the most comprehensive speech.'" (344/474-475)

(I.4) According to another famous hadith, the Prophet (pbuh) prayed to be able to see things as they really are. Mulla Sadra explains that the above features of prophethood all derive from seeing things as they really are, and that since the *awliyā* are completely connected to the Prophet (pbuh), they share in this knowledge to a large extent. These sorts of powers can be found to a much more limited extent, in certain cases where someone sees the future in a dream, or when someone becomes subject to the influence of evil spirits. In the former case, the soothsayer is able to see future physical events; and in the latter case, a body is dominated by spirits other than its own. Even more ordinary is what happens when an impressionable person comes under the influence of someone else and is dominated by them. In such cases, there is a spiritual domination over the physical activity and, hence, the body of another, without any physical force. Sometimes the look of another is enough for a person to come under the other's spell, as it were. In the case of the prophets, such powers are so intense that they obtain knowledge of the entire universe and the entire universe comes under their control.[31] Mulla Sadra concludes that ordinary people, since they are dominated by their material needs, pay the most attention to the miracles and wonders of the prophets and *awliyā*, since miracles and wonders pertain to domination over the material world, and they neglect the special status of the prophets with respect to the imaginary world and the intellectual world. The people of intellect, however, are most impressed with the prophets' stature with regards to the intellectual world, then the imaginary world, and lastly the sensory world. The first status is shown through goodness and virtue. (344-345/474-476)

As mentioned above, section (I.5) is about the qualities of the prophetic warnings; and (I.6) is on the differences among revelation, inspiration, and learning.

(I.7) This section is on the nature of the union of the Prophet (pbuh) and the world of revelation. Mulla Sadra explains that at each of the three domains of sense, imagination and intellect, God has created appropriate realities, each in accordance with a plan that exists in His knowledge, and He has given human beings appropriate faculties to perceive some of the realities at these three levels. At all three levels, human cognition occurs with the union of the faculty of the knower with the form of the reality at the corresponding level. Since the intellectual domain is atemporal, none of the realities at that level can be said to change, and are written on the "protected tablet" (*lawḥ al-maḥfūẓ*).

> "Just as the engineer makes a plan of the form of the building of a house, then carries it out to existence, so too, the Originator of the heavens and the earth writes a plan according to His mercy, and carries it out from the first to the last in the world, through the acting angels that are at the service of the knowing angels. When the existence of the world is finished in its form, Allah created humans from clay and willed to make a *khalifah* (vicegerent, steward) from them in the world and a deputy in the final abode. So He granted the human faculties and consciousness, which are the organs of sense, imagination, and intellect. When one perceives the form of the world, that external form produces another sensory form, and from the sensory form comes another imaginary form." (350/481-482)

Mulla Sadra goes on to explain that this process continues with the formation of an intellectual form, whereby "there is acquired in the intellect the realities (*ḥaqāyiq*) of things that enter into the senses and the imagination." (350-482)

> "What is obtained in the human intellect agrees with the world that exists in the human soul. The world of being corresponds to the copy of existence that is in the intellectual tablet. What is in the intellectual tablet are the hearts of the seraphim (the nearest angels [to God]), and this is prior to its existence in the tablet of destiny (*lawh al-qadarī*), and prior to its existence as a corporeal being. The reverse of this order is the sensory existence, followed by the imaginary and then the

intellectual, I mean, its existence in the intellectual faculty." (350-351/482)

Mulla Sadra then reminds his readers of his epistemological theory about the union of the intellect with what is known through intelligence, and likewise the union of what is sensed with the sensory faculty, and the union of the imaginary with the imagination. When a human being reaches the divine station (*al-maqām al-rabbānī*), everything that is in the divine decree and destiny appears for him. He witnesses the Pen and the Tablet, that is, the intellectual world and the world of the soul.

There are no changes to the Protected Tablet or the realm of the intellect. Only the lower realms are subject to change, and since the divine laws given to the various prophets differed from one another, it can be concluded that the divine laws are not in the intellectual realm, but in the imaginary realm. The divine law is recorded in the Tablet of Erasure and Recording (*lawḥ al-maḥw wa al-ithbāt*). It should be noted that the changes in divine law do not overturn what came before. They are due to changes in circumstance, which make certain rulings inapplicable. What is revealed at the imaginary level is a temporal reflection of the realities that exist timelessly at the intellectual level. What is revealed to the prophets are the forms recorded in the Tablet of Erasure and Recording. All of the judgments of the law have reasons behind them, and these reasons have other reasons behind them that go back to definitive divine judgments and ultimately to the divine names. One who understands how the divine realities of the intellectual forms are reflected in the imaginary world in the way that the prophets can, would not make even the slightest mistake in how this becomes manifest in the world of plurality and change.

(I.8) Although what is in the intellectual world does not change, situations can arise in which the divine decree appears to change. This is because the human understanding of the decree depends upon the changeable conditions in which it is understood.

(I.9) This section explains how the prophet is situated on the border between the world of intellect and the sensory world. It opens with the following observation:

> "Verily the human heart, which is of the rational soul, is like a throne on which mercy is seated, like the Throne on which the Merciful is seated. It is an open gate toward the celestial kingdom (*malakūt*), which is the realm of the protected tablet, the source for the knowing and acting angels, as mentioned, and an open gate toward the faculties of perception and motion." (355/486-487)

The prophets, whose hearts are the purest of all humanity, have clear access to the divine realm from which they receive revelation, and to the realm of God's creatures, to whom they show God's mercy. These are the most perfect levels of humanity and the first conditions for a person to be an apostle of God. In addition, the prophets have been granted the power of speech and excellence of imagination so that they can make use of all they are taught by God for the sake of guiding and directing people toward felicity so that they learn to perform those actions that benefit them. They are also granted polemical skills with which they are able to show the people the invalidity of disbelief.

(I.10) Mulla Sadra claims that there are twelve essential attributes of the Prophet (pbuh).

(i) Excellent understanding, such that he understands everything that he hears and what is said to him as intended by the speaker with the utmost illumination of intellect and light of the soul.

(ii) Memory, so that he never forgets, and his soul is united with the protected tablet.

(iii) A sound nature and balanced temperament.

(iv) Eloquence and good speech without having been taught or receiving any human instruction.

(v) Love of knowledge and wisdom, and mastery of them without exertion, effort or study.

(vi) Disposition not to follow lusts and desires.

(vii) Greatness of soul and nobility, and a distaste for all that is ugly and base, which he would only put up with as a kind of spiritual discipline.

(viii) Love and kindness toward the creatures of God, so that he would never display wrath; and yet without denying the divine punishments.

(ix) A brave heart and no fear of death.

(x) Generous and never stingy because he knew that the divine bounties are inexhaustible.

(xi) The most blissful of all creatures in solitude with God, because he is an *'ārif* (knower of God) to the highest degree.

(xii) Not strict and insistent. He invites people to establish justice and fairness in an easy way. He is, however, strict and insistent in opposing injustice and refuses to accept oppression.

Mulla Sadra ends this section by pointing out how rare it is for someone to be able to combine all these attributes. There are very few temperaments that could maintain such virtues, just as very few are able to attain knowledge of God at the degree of entering into the divine sanctuary. Thus Mulla Sadra finishes the first part of his discussion of prophethood and *wilāyah*. The second part begins with a discussion of how to prove that the prophetic claim is true.

(II.1) Mulla Sadra starts off with comments about the tradition of Ibn Sina to the effect that human beings need to live in societies. These societies must be governed by law in order to prevent oppression and maintain order. Since God has mercy on His creatures, He should provide them with guidance through a law by means of which they can live in peace and draw closer to Him. This law can only be brought to human beings through a prophet. The prophetic guides must be of a fitting stature and have the virtues to guide individuals and communities to felicity in both this world and the next. As such, the prophets are human manifestations of divine mercy.

(II.2) The prophet should prescribe rules of conduct and worship for the people so that they may be led from the condition of being like animals to that of being like angels. The benefits of various forms of worship are mentioned.

(II.3) This world is a place in which human beings set out on a journey towards God. The journey has many stations, from the material, through the various vegetative and animalistic stations, to the stations of humanity, and finally to the angelic. In this journey, some are more advanced than others. The prophets are those who are the most advanced on this way, and who can therefore lead others toward God. For this purpose, (to establish an order with justice and security within the framework of which people can live and worship and advance their own spiritual journey), political arrangements and punishments are established by divine law.

(II.4) Mulla Sadra opens this section with a comparison:

> "The relation of prophethood to the *sharīʻah* is like the relation of the spirit to the body in which the spirit is, and politics without religion (or divine

law, *shar'*) is like the body in which there is no spirit." (364/496)

He goes on to explain that while some so-called philosophers have claimed that there is no difference between politics and *sharī'ah*, the difference is affirmed in Plato's *Laws* and elaborates on how they differ. For Mulla Sadra, *sharī'ah* means the rule of divine law and is contrasted with *politics* which he takes to be rule for individual interests.

(II.5) Continuing the Platonic theme, Mulla Sadra asserts that just as man is divided into three faculties, rational, imaginary, and sensory, so too, the people that make up a society may be divided into corresponding groups. The secret to understanding the rules of the *sharī'ah* is that they all serve to lead man through successively higher levels.

The next three sections, (II.6), (II.7), and (II.8), are about particular acts of worship, sin, and different aspects of the divine law, or sharī'ah, respectively. In the final section (II.9), Mulla Sadra concludes that although prophethood has been discontinued with the passing away of the Prophet Muḥammad (pbuh), in the sense that no one after him is to be called a prophet or receive revelation brought by the angel Gabriel as it is for the Prophet, there is a sense in which it continues. God continues to inspire the Imams and others following them to lead people in the right way towards Him.

V. The Prophet Muhammad (pbuh) in 'Irfān

The Sufis, generally speaking, take the same sort of view of prophethood and in particular of the Prophet Muḥammad (pbuh), as the Shi'a. For both sects, the status of the prophets is exalted, and the existence of Prophet Muhammad (pbuh) is given metaphysical significance. In this regard we might consider the famous Sufi poet, Farīd al-Dīn 'Aṭṭār (d. c. 1221). Although it is believed that ‘Aṭṭār followed Sunni jurisprudence (Hanafi), his praises of the first three Caliphs as well as the Shi‘ite Imams Bāqir and Ṣādiq have confused scholars with regard to his confessional loyalties.

In his *Book of God* (*Ilāhī Nāmah*),[32] ‘Attar begins, as is customary, with praising God and honoring the Prophet. The section on the Prophet is too long to quote here, but more than a few passages are worth quoting or summarizing. The section begins as follows:

> "Muhammad is the exemplar to both worlds, the guide of the descendants of Adam.
>
> He is the sun of creation, the moon of the celestial spheres, the all-seeing eye;
>
> The torch of knowledge, the candle of prophecy, the lamp of the nation and the way of the people;
>
> The commander-in-chief on the parade-ground of the Law; the general of the army of mysteries and morals;
>
> The lord of the world and the glory of the ‘But for thee’;[33] ruler of the earth and of the celestial spheres;
>
> The most loyal of the Prophets, the proof of the Way, the king without a seal, the sultan without a crown.
>
> As a king he reared up a lofty palace, but he followed the principle of ‘Poverty is my pride.’[34] (6)
>
> ...

He, and only he, is without question the most excellent of mankind; he and he only, is the confident of God.

The seven heavens and the eight gardens of paradise were created for him; he is both the eye and the light in the light of our eyes. (6)

…

With his mind [*fekresh*, literally, his thought] he solved the difficulties of all mankind for his mind had seen the first design in Eternity Past. (7)

…

He was indeed the culmination of the Prophets; when he came, the Prophecy was complete.

Hast thou not seen how first the army comes and then the noble King arrives.

The Prophets are like the army; they came only to announce the king.

When the sultan of Prophecy was born, the Prophecy came to an end for he was the culmination thereof. (7)

…

Without love for him the heavens cannot revolve; without their longing for him the angels cannot breathe.

The Faith itself could have nothing without his support; no eye ever saw him knit his brow.

> He was pure contentment with no feeling of anger; no eye ever saw him frown. (8)
>
> ...
>
> When he returned, with a hundred honors, from his ascension [mi'rāj], his face never grew dark.
>
> His stars relate that when he sat like the moon in their company,
>
> He eclipsed that company with a light such as that with which the sun eclipses a candle..." (10)

There is a lyrical account of the mi'rāj that goes on for several pages. With reference to the "two bow lengths" mentioned in the Qur'an: *"Then he drew nearer and nearer until he was within two bow lengths or even nearer"*, 'Aṭṭār comments:

> "When, in the first place, he set out towards God, he sped upwards like an arrow from the bow.
>
> And when, in the end, he was sent back to mankind, he was discharged like an arrow from the bow.
>
> These two flights were from two bows, hence the parable of the 'two bows'.
>
> And since Sagittarius is always in two houses, therefore there are always two parts to that bow.
>
> One thou knowest as that of Aḥad [unity], and the other is that of the eternal Aḥmad [Muhammad].
>
> The attraction of God shot forth like an arrow and split the *mīm* of Aḥmad in two like a hair.

> The *mīm* of Aḥmad fell out and it became Aḥad; and all duality became unity. (16)
>
> ...
>
> "God, Who to glorify Adam revealed to him the names of all things,
>
> Revealed to Muhammad the things themselves and therefore made him illiterate and poor.
>
> Going beyond names to the nameless state of things he had no need to read and was therefore illiterate.
>
> Since he went disembodied along the road of God he became from disembodiment absolutely poor..." (17)

'Aṭṭār finishes his exordium to the Prophet with a story, according to which there was once a prostitute who came to the Prophet (pbuh) and asked for a gift. She complimented the Prophet (pbuh), and he gave her his only cloak and asked his friends to each give her something. The result was that she became rich. 'Aṭṭār continues, addressing the Prophet (pbuh):

> "Since the woman had a cloak from thee, I too should have a present.
>
> Thou art king in both worlds and canst bestow divine robes of honor.
>
> Honor his body with such a robe of which even his shirt will not be aware.
>
> Adorn his heart with a belief in God's oneness such as cannot enter a specific body.

> All that I seek is disembodiment, but why do I speak seeing that thou knowest and art able?..." (20)

One of the scholars most famous for his explicit avowal of both the Sufi path and the Shi'ite denomination was Sayyid Haydar Amuli (d. c. 1391), who studied under 'Allāmah Ḥillī's son, himself a great scholar, known as Fakhr al-Muḥaqiqin (d. 1369). In his *Secrets of the Path (Asrār al-Shari'ah)*[35] he discusses each of the various elements of the Shi'ite creed and practice from three perspectives: the exoteric view, *shari'ah;* the esoteric view, *ṭarīqah;* and finally, the ultimate view, *ḥaqīqah.* The discussion of prophethood is preceded by a short introduction that affirms the philosophical view that the prophets receive knowledge from God "by means of the essence of the First Intellect, known sometimes as Gabriel and sometimes as the Holy Spirit." (109)

In his review of prophethood, according to the people of *shari'ah,* he states that prophethood is recognized by three features: (1) the rationality of what he establishes in word and deed; (2) his call for obedience to God; and (3) miracles. He also discusses how God's kindness obliges Him to send prophets for human guidance, and the infallibility of the prophets.

In his summary of prophethood according to the people of *ṭarīqah,* Sayyid Haydar sounds a philosophical note in the following passage:

> "The prophetic mission is an expression of the special treatment of man by God. This special relationship issues from Him by means of His revelation. This revelation is in the form of those divine emanations or unveilings which cause the bringing into being of the source-forms in the realm of knowledge; these emanations are also known as the most sacred divine outpourings." (112)

When he turns to prophethood from the perspective of the people of the truth (*ḥaqīqah*), Sayyid Haydar Amuli writes:

> "Know that the prophethood of this group is an expression of the good news or revelation from the divine: the prophet is the one who is informed of the Essence of Allah and of His Attributes, His Names, His laws and His wishes. The real and essential prophetic announcement is nothing other than that. The Greater Spirit was sent by Allah to the First Universal Soul and from there to the particular individual soul in order to inform it in the language of intellect, of the Unity of Essence, the Attributes from before endless time, the divine Names, the illustrious laws and His revered will. Every prophet from Adam to Muhammad is a manifestation of the various manifestations of the prophethood of the Greater Spirit: the prophethood of the latter is essential and eternal; the prophethood of the various other manifestations is incidental and interrupted - except that of the prophethood of Muhammad whose prophethood is eternal and uninterrupted since his reality is the reality of the Greater Spirit and his form includes the various forms in which this reality manifests. The rest of the prophets manifest by means of some of the names and qualities: each manifestation is an emanation of one of the qualities, or one of the names, except that of the Muhammadi manifestation which emanates from the essence of the Greater Spirit and by means of all its qualities. Moreover, in this manifestation prophethood comes to a close. The Messenger, (may Allah bless him and his family), preceded all the prophets with respect to the reality of prophethood, yet comes after them with respect to outward form. He himself has said: 'We are the

> last and the first' and also 'I was a prophet when Adam was (in a state) between water and clay.'" (113-114)

This last hadith is also emphasized in the treatment of prophethood by Muḥsin Fayḍ Kāshānī (d. 1680) in his *Kalimāt-e Maknūneh (Hidden Words).*[36] Fayḍ also explicitly describes prophethood in terms of the Sufi concept of the perfect man (*insān al-kāmil*).

> "The perfect man is either a prophet or a saint, and each of these has two respects, the respect of absoluteness and the respect of being restricted, that is, general and specific. Absolute prophethood is real prophethood obtained in pre-eternity and remaining until post-eternity. It is the prophet's consciousness, exclusive to he who has absolute prophethood, of the capacities of all existence according to their essences, and his ability to grant the rights of everything that has a right. It is in this regard that this prophethood is called the greatest lordship and the major sovereignty. One who has this position is called the greatest vicegerent, the pole of poles, the great man, the real Adam, is referred to as the highest pen, the first intellect and the greatest spirit. There is reference to this in his (pbuh) saying, 'The first thing that Allah created was my light,' and 'I was a prophet when Adam was between water and clay,' and others of this sort. All knowledge and practice depends on him, and ultimately all levels and stages, whether of prophethood or sainthood, of an apostle or executor, lead to him.
>
> The interior of this prophethood is absolute sainthood (wilāyah), which is the obtaining of all these perfections esoterically from pre-eternity and

their remaining until post-eternity. This returns to the annihilation of the servant in *al-Ḥaqq* and his persistence in Him, and there is an indication of this in his saying, 'I and 'Alī are from a single light,' and 'Allah created my spirit and the spirit of 'Alī ibn Abī Ṭālib two thousand years before He created people, and He raised 'Alī with every prophet secretly, but with me openly.' This is also indicated by the saying of the Commander of the Faithful (a.s.), 'I was a saint when Adam was between water and clay,' and others of the same sort. (167)

Restricted prophethood is being given information about divine realities, that is, gnosis of the essence of *al-Ḥaqq* and His names, attributes, and precepts. If added to this is the propagation of the precepts, training people in morals, teaching them wisdom and taking a political stand, then this is legislative prophethood, only for an apostle. Parallel to this is restricted sainthood. Insofar as prophethood and sainthood are divine attributes, they are absolute, and insofar as they are based on the prophets and the saints, they are restricted. The restricted is based on the absolute, and the absolute is manifest in the restricted." (168)

Fayḍ goes on to explain that the prophethood of each of the prophets is a particular instance of absolute prophethood, and that the seal of both absolute and restricted prophethood, beyond which there is no further level of prophethood, is Muḥammad (pbuh). He quotes the following hadith to confirm this point: "A parable for prophethood is that of a house built with only one brick missing, and I am that brick."

The discussion continues with an elaboration of the concept of the Prophet as the supreme instance of the perfect man whose reality (*ḥaqīqah*) is the form of the One.

> "The root and source, return and origin of all creatures is reality of all realities, and that is Muḥammad, (a reality) and the Aḥmadian light, which is the form of the Unitary One. It includes all divine and cosmic perfections, and is the setter of the scales of all the levels for angelic, animal and human temperance. The world and its inhabitants are the form and parts of his elaboration. Adam and humans are subordinate to him for his perfection. This is indicated by his (pbuh) words, "I am the master of the children of Adam," and by his words, "Adam and those who came after are under my banner." (168)

> "There is no intermediary between him and *al-Ḥaqq*, mighty is His sovereignty, as he said, 'The first thing that Allah created was my spirit (or my light),' and he is the goal of all actions, as He said, 'If it were not for you, I would not have created the celestial spheres.'" (169)

Fayḍ continues that our Prophet is the most perfect of all creatures, even considering the Imams and *awliyā* (saints), who are, "after him [Muhammad], the best creatures and the most perfect creatures, especially the Commander of the Faithful [Imam 'Alī]." (169)

VI. The Prophet Muhammad (pbuh) as Absolute Prophet

Although we have divided the discussions of the Prophet (pbuh) in religious texts, doctrinal statements, and books on philosophy and *'irfān*, the division is somewhat artificial, for the boundaries in these fields are porous, and many individuals throughout Shi'ite history have displayed a perspective that synthesizes what is found in all these different areas. So, for example, Naṣīr al-Dīn Ṭūsī and Jamāl al-Dīn Ḥillī both wrote works of dogmatic theology, philosophy, and *'irfān,*[37] and Mulla Sadra and his son-in-law, Fayḍ Kāshānī wrote works in the areas of Qur'anic interpretation, theological works, philosophy and *'irfān*. So, the divisions we have made among the texts considered should not be understood as indicating different factions among the Shi'a, but rather different textual traditions that often merge.

In the course of the history of these textual traditions, there is a movement towards idealization. The Prophet Muhammad (pbuh) is understood as the climaxing personification of the theory of prophethood as elaborated over the course of the centuries. This is not to deny or oppose the historical person or idealize him, for there was a single person who appears in history who was orphaned and raised by an uncle and experienced all the details of the life of the famous religious leader of Arabia, some six hundred years after Christ. However, at the same time, he is one who was appointed by God and given the mission of warning and bearing the glad tidings of divine mercy and sovereignty, and he is the same person who is the pure light of God's first creation and for the sake of whom the entire world has been created. In Shi'ite thought, these are not to be understood as opposing paradigms, but as different hierarchically ordered aspects of a single reality. The lowest level of such aspects is that of the Arabian man's physical history, his movements and what he ate. At a higher level, there is the person Muhammad as prophet and an apostle of God, the recipient of divine revelation, and the divine guide. Finally, there is Muhammad as the light of intellect, pure illumination and virtue, a cosmic reality totally annihilated in divinity. This division is reflected in Haydar Āmuli's division of *shari'at*, *tariqat,* and *haqiqat*, and in Mulla Sadra's division of the sensory, imaginary, and intellectual worlds.

As we have seen, Muslim writers often divide their discussions about prophethood into general discussions, (what it means to be a prophet), and specific discussions, (the prophethood of Muhammad), or as Fayḍ Kāshānī puts it, about absolute compared with restricted prophethood. As Fayḍ writes, "The restricted is based on the absolute, and the absolute is manifest in the restricted." In the Prophet Muḥammad (pbuh), however, the instance and the universal paradigm are united in one, in a manner analogous to Plato's early theory of the forms as perfect paradigms. The only difference is that for Plato, the paradigm could never exist as a concrete embodiment of reality because material existence was itself seen as contrary to the ideality of the forms. In Shi'ite thought, on the other hand, there is a single reality that is at once material and immaterial, corporeal and non-corporeal, but at different levels of its existence.

The prophets come as guides to show the path towards God. This also occurs on several levels, the way of the outward law, *sharī'ah*, the inward way of the *ṭariqah*, and the fully realized way of the truth, *ḥaqīqah*. All three of these levels are brought to completion by the Prophet Muhammad (pbuh), although in different ways. With respect to the law, he is the final prophet to bring a divine law and book. With him the succession of prophets comes to an end, but divine guidance continues through the succession of the Imams. God completes His religion through Muḥammad (pbuh) when the Qur'an has been revealed and Muḥammad (pbuh) has announced the divine appointment of 'Alī (a.s.). These two "weighty things" (*thaqalayn*), the Qur'an and the household of the Prophet, are like two points that determine a line that extends toward the realization or *ḥaqīqah*, indicated by "the Pond" (*kawthar*), in accordance with the famous hadith in which the Prophet (pbuh) is reported to have said:

> "Verily, I am leaving behind two weighty things among you: the Book of God and my kindred (*'itrah*), my household (*Ahl al-Bayt*), for indeed, the two will never separate until they come back to

me by the Pond (of *al-Kawthar* on the Judgement Day)."[38]

The series of divine prophets includes those who brought divine law, which is the exoteric aspect of *dīn* (religion in the sense of divine guidance). With the passing away of the Prophet (pbuh), not only did the individual pass away, but the entire series of prophets also came to an end. Universal or absolute prophethood is in this way, too, united with the individual prophethood of Muḥammad (pbuh). The esoteric aspect of his mission and the mission of prophethood in general, however, continues through the series that constitutes the Imamate, for the Prophet (pbuh) was not only prophet, but a *walī*, too; and it is his *walāyah* that continues through the sequence of Imamate. According to some Shi'ite narrations, the Pond is also a symbol for the Prophet's daughter, Fāṭimah (a.s.), the wife of Imam 'Alī (a.s.). Her position as daughter and wife makes her the link that joins prophethood and Imamate, the exoteric and the esoteric. The ultimate realization is the offspring of the exoteric and the spouse of the esoteric. This relationship between the external, the interior and realization, however, are not merely abstract speculations, for they speak directly to the establishment and spiritual direction of the religious community. Hence, the narration of *thaqalayn* is not merely descriptive; rather it is guidance to the believers, that they should cling to the divine book revealed to the Prophet Muḥammad (pbuh) and the leadership of the Imams that he announced at Ghadīr (and other places) in order to approach the Kingdom of God on Judgement Day.

The Prophet Muḥammad (pbuh) can be considered the absolute prophet not only because absolute prophethood is manifest in him, but because each of the levels of prophethood achieves fulfillment in him, since it is through his life, revelation and designation of the Imamate that he makes manifest his own spiritual ascent and invites the believers to take up the quest themselves as individuals and as a community.

[1] Fayd Kāshānī, *Al-Mahjat al-Baydā fī Tahdhīb al-Ihiyā,* (Qom: Daftar-e Intishārāt Islāmī, 1415AH/1994AD), Vol. 4, p.118.

[2] It is strongly recommended that a short prayer of benediction should be said whenever the Prophet is mentioned: "May the blessings and peace of Allah be granted to him and to his progeny." This is abbreviated here to '(pbuh)': peace be upon him. Note that the phase "and to his progeny" is specific to the Shi'a.

[3] See Qur'ān, Baqarah, 2:31.

[4] See Sachiko Murata and William C. Chittick, *The Vision of Islam* (New York: Paragon House, 1994), ch. 4, pp.132-137.

[5] *Kanz al-'Ummāl*, hadith no. 5217.

[6] For a review of the sources and variations on this narration see URL = [illegible].

[7] Isra, 17:1; Najm, 53:1-21; Takwir, 81:19-25.

[8] The most important such narrations in the Shi'i collections have been gathered by Muḥsin Fayḍ Kāshānī, the translation of which may be found at URL = http://www.al-islam.org/al-miraj/.

[9] Page references will be given to the English translation of Jafar Husain (Qom: Ansariyan, 1989) in the following form: (S xx/yy: nn), where xx is the sermon number and nn is the page number in the Ansariyan edition, and yy is the sermon number in the web edition: http://www.al-islam.org/nahj/.

[10] Shaykh Ṣadūq, *A Shi'ite Creed,* tr. Asaf A. A. Fyzee (Tehran: WOFIS, 1982), p.81.

[11] Shaykh Ṣadūq (1982), p.145.

[12] Shaykh Ṣadūq (1982), p. 84.

[13] Ibid. p. 87.

[14] See Martin J. McDermott, *The Theology of Shaikh Al-Mufīd* (d. 413AH/1022AD) (Beirut: Dar el-Machreq, 1986), p. 99ff.

[15] 'Allāmah Ḥillī, *Kashf al-Murād fī Tajrīd al-I'tiqād* (Qom: Mu'assissah Nashr Islamī, 1404AH/1984AD), pp.346-360.

[16] Ja'far Sobhani, *Doctrines of Shi'i Islam* (London: I. B. Tauris, 2001), pp.61-96.

[17]Ayatullah Muḥammad Taqī Miṣbāḥ Yazdī, *Āmūzesh-e I'tiqād* (Tehran: Sāzmān-e Tablīghāt-e Islamī, 1374AH/1995AD).

[18] F. Rahman, *Prophecy in Islam* (London: George Allen & Unwin, 1958), p. 14.

[19] See Henry Corbin, *Avicenna and the Visionary Recital* (Irving: Spring Publications, 1980).

[20] W. M. Thackston, *The Mystical and Visionary Treatises of Shihabuddin Yahya Suhrawardi* (London: Octagon, 1982).

[21] A translation of the essay along with an argument in favor of the attribution of it to Ibn Sina may be found in Peter Heath, *Allegory and Philosophy in Avicenna (Ibn Sīnā): With a Translation of the Book of the Prophet Muhammad's Ascent to Heaven* (Philadelphia: University of Pennsylvania Press, 1992). Additional evidence of Ibn Sina's being a Shi'ite is that all the names of his household that are known were popular among the Shi'ah. See Arthur J. Arberry, *Avicenna on Theology* (Westport: Hyperion, 1979), p.5.

[22] Corbin (1980), p.251.

[23] Henry Corbin, *Spiritual Body and Celestial Earth* (Princeton: Princeton University Press, 1977), pp.318 n. 8; 282-283 n. 76.

[24] Fārābī, *Taḥṣīl al-Sa'ādah* (Haydarabad: 1345AH), p.40, cited in Rahman (1958), p.61.

[25] Corbin (1980), p.166.

[26] See Rahman (1958), pp.52-64, who traces elements of this sort of approach to Plato and to the Stoics.

[27] Ibn Sina, *Najāt* (Cairo: 1938), p.10, cited in Rahman (1958), p.55. Rahman sees the ultimate conflict between the philosophers and the "orthodox" lying in the contrary ideals of contemplation and activism. However, this only describes orthodoxy as developed in Sunni *kalām*; for the Shi'ah (and Heath's arguments for the authenticity of Ibn Sina's *Mi'raj Nama* provide evidence for his Shi'ism, as well), the contemplative and the active goals are by no means opposed; just as justice and wisdom are not opposed. Compare the opposition described by Rahman (1958), p.64 and110, with the views described below of Sayyid Haydar 'Āmulī, Mulla Sadra, and Fayḍ Kāshānī.

[28] Ṣadr al-Dīn Shīrāzī, *Al-Shawāhid al-Rubūbiyah* (Mashhad: Mashhad University Press, 1346AH/1967AD). I have also benefited from the Persian translation of this work by Javād Mosleh (Tehran: Soroush Press, 1996). Page references will be given in the form (n/m) where n is the page number of the Arabic text and m is the page number of the Persian translation.

[29] The term *wilāyah* means both *guardianship* (of the other believers) and *authority*, and is closely related to the term *walāyah*, signifying love (of the Ahl al-Bayt). The prophets and Imams are said to be *awliyah* (sing. *walī*), meaning that they have divine authority, and that they are the special friends of God. Orientalists often translate this as "sainthood".

[30] Here Mulla Sadra refers to the verse of light in the Qur'an, (Noor, 24:35).

[31] The position taken here with regard to occult influences is a development of discussions of this topic that can be found in Ibn Sina (*Ishārāt*), as explained in Rahman (1958), p.51.

[32] All quotations are from Farīd al-Dīn 'Aṭṭār, *The Ilāhī-nāma or Book of God*, tr. John Andrew Boyle (Manchester: Manchester University Press, 1976); page numbers will be given in parentheses after the quoted text.

[33] This refers to the hadith according to which God said to Muhammad, "But for thee, I would not have created the heavens."

[34] This is a well known hadith.

[35]Sayyid Haydar Amuli, *Inner Secrets of the Path* (Longmead: Element Books, 1989). Page numbers will be given after quoted text from this translation.

[36] Muḥsin Fayḍ Kāshānī, *Kalimāt-e Maknūneh* (Qom: Maṭbū'āt-e Dīnī, 1386AH/2007AD). Page references for my translations will be given to the original Persian/Arabic text of this edition.

[37] See the discussion of such connections by Seyyed Hossein Nasr, "Shi'ism and Sufism: their relationship in essence and in history," in his *Sufi Essays,* 2nd ed. (Albany: SUNY, 1991), pp.104-120.

[38] For a discussion of the variations on this hadith, and their narrators, see URL = (accessed 1 February 2009).

Subjects of Love According to the Prophet Muhammad

Abbas Ali Shameli

قال رسول الله صلي الله عليه و آله و سلم: "حبّب إليّ من دنياكم ثلاث: النّساء و الطّيب و جعلت قرّة عيني في الصّلوة".

The Prophet Muhammad (S) said: "From your world, three things are made lovable and attractive to me: women, fragrance and my utmost pleasure, which is prayer."[1]

Different approaches can be used to understand the Prophet's words. These include literal, theological, traditional, mystical and even socio and psychological approaches. In this paper, the different versions of the hadith as it is narrated in Shi'i and Sunni sources will be compared using a theological approach based on the verbal differences between the versions. The paper will then close with a quick look at Ibn Arabi's mystical interpretation of this hadith in the last chapter of his *Fusus*.

I. Ghazali's Version of the Prophet's Saying

This maxim is recorded by Abu Hamid al-Ghazali (450-505AH/1057-1111AD) in his interesting discussion in *Kitāb al-Mahabbah* (The Book of Love). Ghazali's main concern is to explain the real nature and various types of love and the stages in its process of formation in order to highlight the final stage of love, devotion to God.

Defining love (*mahabbah*) as something that incorporates both perception and pleasure: *"la ma'nā li al-hubb illā al-mayl ilā mā fi idrākihi ladhdhah*", meaning "there is no meaning for love except a tendency to conceive something which brings pleasure" (Ghazali, *Ihyā',* p. 254). Ghazali argues that a person may divide perception and pleasure based on his/her different senses. Each sense deals with a specific type of sensibilia and of course, a particular type of pleasure. Accordingly, he quotes the above mentioned narration as proof for his argument. He asserts that in the Prophet's words, each of the three terms, women (*nisā'*), perfume (*ṭīb*) and prayer (*salāh*), are associated with one or more of the senses. A perfume is desired because we perceive its aroma through our sense of smell and not through seeing and/or hearing it. Women, on the other hand, are beloved since we enjoy them through touch and by seeing and talking to them. It follows that other senses such as smell, taste and hearing are not foremost in our enjoyment of women. Prayer is considered the most desirable act because it is perceived through our hearts and minds.

Ghazali therefore points out that according to this maxim of the Prophet, we must use our inner senses as well as our external ones to help us enjoy the inner meanings of divine truths as they pertain to God.

Although it can be reasonable to divide perception (or more precisely sensation) and pleasure into two categories, one may also argue that it is problematic to use the Prophet's saying as an example of this doctrine. Women, for instance, are not only lovable because we enjoy being with them and derive pleasure from them primarily through the senses of touch and sight. If one wants to understand the real reason that the Prophet has mentioned these three items in his saying then one should refer to the holy Qur'an and other Prophetic sayings. It is important to know and to realize that besides their physical and physiological aspects, women are also considered to be the main source of satisfaction for psychological needs, particularly in the family unit. According to verse 30:21 of the holy Qur'an, wife is the main sources of tranquillity and relaxation. In one of Imam Riḍa (A.S)'s sayings, he says that in same way that God has made night a source of tranquillity He has made women also a source of tranquillity.[2] The release of tension that a woman can provide is not rooted in the senses of sight and touch alone. It is a psychological need which is met through inter-relationships between a wife and a husband. In another verse of the holy Qur'an (33:32), which is particularly addressed to the Prophet's wives, God instructs that they should not make their voices soft so as to excite a person to feel an eager desire for them:

> ".. be not too complaisant of speech, lest one in whose heart is a disease should be moved with desire."

Although the verse is addressed to the Prophet's wives, this instruction can be generalized to include every woman since there is no specific address in the verse. Accordingly, a woman's voice (even if she is not singing) might be a source of pleasure for men. This shows that we may take benefit from women through the sense of hearing too.

In addition, Imam Ali (A.S) says that women are like flowers[3] so they must not be used for physically demanding work or be put under emotional or mental pressure. Even though the Imam said that they are like flowers in the sense that they are not to be misused for hard work, one may also come to the conclusion that they are fragrant like flowers and should be smelled. Thus we may enjoy them through our sense of smell. Based on his mystical approach, Ibn Arabi states that perfume *(al-tib)* is mentioned after the term women *(al-nisā)* since in women there are existential odours.[1] As it is said in a famous Arabic saying: "The best scent is (what is on) the beloved's neck".[2]

II. Verbal Differences

Before discussing the verbal differences in the various versions of the Prophet's saying, we have to consider the importance of the utilisation of the passive form of "*hubbiba*". The fact that the three things mentioned are 'made lovable' to the Prophet implies that his tendency to favour the three subjects mentioned is something that was bestowed on him by God. Thus it is God Who created us with a system of desires and dislikes. This idea is not only mentioned in the holy Qur'an[3] but appears explicitly in other versions of the hadith as well. One of these literal differences in the hadith is the term "*dunyā*" (this world).

Although Ghazali uses a version of this hadith that contains the term "*al-dunyā*", the original sources from which he quotes are different. In both Shi'i and Sunni sources there are three versions concerning this term. Sometimes it appears as "*min al-dunyā*"[4] sometimes as "*min dunyākum*"[5] and occasionally "*dunyā*" is not used at all.[6] A problem arises if We take into account the term "*dunyā*" in its two forms: "*dunyākum*" or "*al-dunyā*". One may argue that despite the fact that the first two things mentioned, namely women and perfume, are worldly affairs, prayer, surely, cannot be considered as such. So how can they all be put together in one context as worldly issues?!

There are two possible answers to this question. One is to use the version of the hadith that lacks the term "*dunyā*". The other is Suyuti's suggestion, according to which there is an alternative meaning for the word "*min*". He asserts that according to Tustari in *Sharh al-Arba'in* "*min*" in this hadith means "*fi*". So, all three cases would be considered religious matters "*min al-din*" even though they are in the world "*fi al-dunyā*".[7] Interestingly we should note that "*min dunyākum*" implies that the Prophet essentially did not have any tendency towards worldly affairs. This was because he was completely devoted to God. However as a role model he behaved in such a way that his followers took him as a perfect example and so behaved in a moderate and balanced manner as well.[8] Comparing the content of this Prophet's saying with what is revealed in verse 3:14 of the holy Qur'an[9] we realize that for some people women and sons are only provisions for the life of this world. Surprisingly, in another verse (25:74)[10] both women and offspring are regarded as the most pleasurable "*qurrat 'ayn*", exactly as the Prophet refers to prayer in this hadith. This is achieved if our behaviour is based on piety.

The other verbal difference in sources of the hadith is the existence or non-existence of the term "*thalāth*" (three). With the exception of Ghazali (*Ihyā,* Kitāb al-Mahabbah, p. 255*),* Fayd *(Al-Mahajjah,* Vol. 3, p. 68) and Majlisi in one of his quotations *(Bihār al-Anwār,* Vol. 73, p. 141), none of the other Shi'i or Sunni sources have included the term "*thalāth*"[11] in the Prophet's saying. However, the resulting problem is similar to that encountered when the hadith contains the term "*dunyā*" in that consequently all three cases are put into one category with no differentiation between them. This argument can be counterargued in one of the following ways:

1. Either most of the versions which are quoted by narrationists do not incorporate the term "*thalāth*".

2. If, as suggested by Suyuti, "*min*" means "*fi*", then there will not be any problem, even if we put all three cases into one category.

3. "*Salāt*" is always distinguished by the Prophet with the term "*qurrat 'ayni*" (my utmost pleasure) and is sometimes joined with a new verb, such as "*ju'ila*" or "*ju'ilat*".

4. In other versions of the hadith sometimes only women (*nisā*) and perfume (*tib*) are put together[12] but prayer (*salāat*) is quoted separately[13]. In addition, if they are all put together, they are distinguished verbally.[14]

Another literal argument is about the order of the two terms "*al-nisā*'" and "*al-tib*." Apart from Ghazali (*Ihyā,* kitab al-Mahabbah, Volume 36, p. 255), we find only Fayd (*Al-Mahajjah,* Vol. 3, p. 68) and al-Mutqi (*Kanz al-'Ummāl,* Vol. 6, p. 673) quoting the hadith beginning with "*al-tib*". All other sources give priority to the term "*al-nisā*". I do not believe that this verbal order makes any difference to the meaning of the hadith or that it creates a priority regarding the appeal of the two. However, all Sunni and Shi'i original sources give verbal priority to the term "*al-nisā*".

The final phrase of the Prophet's saying is: **"and my utmost pleasure which is made to be prayer."** Although we are not sure whether this phrase is distinguished by a separate verb or not,[15] there is a huge difference between "*hubbiba*" and "*qurrat 'ayni*". Being a manner by which, or as a consequence of which, the 'eye becomes refreshed' or one achieves a state of deep rest and tranquillity (*al-qarār; al-hudū'*)[16], shows that while praying one is at the apex of meeting his hopes and desires. So, the best kind of pleasure is acquired through performing prayer. Accordingly, even if we take pleasure in women and perfume, which put us in a state of relaxation, our ultimate and most pleasurable tranquillity will be achieved in prayer. It was accordingly that the Prophet said:

> "…the prayer is made as lovable to me as water is to a thirsty person and food is to someone who is hungry. Yet the difference is that they will be

quickly satisfied by drinking and eating but I never become tired of praying."[17]

III. Ibn Arabi's Mystical Interpretation

Quoting the Prophet's saying in the last chapter of his *Fusus al-Hikam,* Ibn Arabi takes an interesting mystical approach. While he considers the hadith a unique bezel, which issued from Prophet Muhammad,[18] Ibn Arabi places emphasis on the word "*hubbiba*". He comes up with the idea that the Prophet started his saying with love, because love is the very core of all of creation.[19] God created man in His form and then He loved him. He also created women from men in their form. So, men existentially tend to love women [20] because they are in fact a part of men's existence.[21] Women consequently tend to love men like someone who likes their hometown and place of origin. Therefore, the Prophet loved women because he observed the true reality found in them.

In addition, Ibn Arabi combines love with his feminist theory with which he offers a new explanation for the manifestation of man in the course of creation. According to Ibn Arabi, the harmony of the items in the Prophet's saying resembles what actually occurs in existence. "*Al-tib*", as a masculine term, is located between "*al-nisā*" (a real feminine term) and "*al-salāt*" (a grammatical feminine term), just as the location of Adam is to be found between the Divine Essence (*al-dhaat al-mawjoud 'anhā* - again a metaphorical feminine), which is the very source of his creation and Eve, (a real feminine), who is manifested from Adam.[22] Therefore, in both cases there is a masculine term surrounded by two feminine terms. Ibn Arabi then explains that mentioning women first and prayer last in the hadith is because the manifestation of a woman's entity is part of man's existence. Man observes the reflection of his existence in woman. In addition, according to the Prophet, self- knowledge always precedes knowing God.[23] So, whenever man wants to know his Lord, he must firstly know himself. Knowing himself partly depends on knowing women since they are indeed the manifestation of his existence.

In an attempt to interpret the last phrase of the Prophet's saying, he argues that prayer is "*qurrat al-'ayn*" since it is seeing and observing (*mushāhadah* & *ru'yah*). So, the utmost pleasure of prayer is for the inner eye. Prayer is the remembrance (*dhikr*) of God and he who remembers the True Reality puts himself in one session with God.[24] Eventually, if one has inner sight, he will undoubtedly observe who sits beside him. If one does not achieve the stage of seeing, then he cannot reach the ultimate reality of prayer and of course, he will not have "*qurrat al-'ayn*". "*Qurrat al-'ayn*" is nothing other than observing the beloved. When a lover sees his beloved, his eyes will be completely satisfied and he will want nothing else. This is why prayer is considered to be something by which, or as a consequence of which, the eye becomes cool, refreshed or completely at rest.

IV. Comments

Comparing Ghazali's approach with that of Ibn Arabi, we realize that the Prophet's saying, like the Holy Qur'an, includes various aspects and can be approached and studied based on different perspectives. However, Ghazali's approach has its own limitations, which were also discussed in this paper. Although both Ghazali and Fayd Kashani quoted this Prophetic hadith from Nassā'i and Ahmad Ibn Hanbal, one can see some differences in the verbal aspects of it, which may change our understanding and the meaning of the hadith.

Combining the love of women and perfume with prayer, the Prophet put forward a moderate model in which both worldly and divine affairs have been taken into proper consideration. Thus, both extremes in attitude and action in relation to these three subjects have been excised from the Prophetic tradition. This means that neither isolating oneself from women and perfume as examples of worldly matters and concerning oneself only with prayer, nor showing interest only in divine issues and withdrawing oneself from the beauties and attractions of this world, can be considered correct according to Prophetic tradition.

The things that the Prophet loved included a balanced range of worldly and divine subjects. However, by utilizing two different terms, one for women and perfume, "*hubbiba*", on the one hand, and another for prayer, "*qurrat 'ayn*", on the other, the Prophet indicated his careful attention to dividing his love properly between both aspects.[25] This is similar to the fact indicated in this hadith that only prayer is the subject of "*qurrat al-'ay*n". Of course, based on the Qur'anic idea and being inspired by devotion to God through prayer, women and offspring can also be the subject of "*qurrat al-'ayn*" if they are loved as paths to piety and perfection.

Another socially important point is the Prophet's opinion that perfume is also a lovable thing, alongside women and prayer. A significant practical characteristic of the Prophet was his use of perfume. He used to spend more money buying perfume than buying food![26] He did not only utilize the perfume for prayer but also when he wanted to visit people or appear in public. On these occasions, he would try to be nicely perfumed. Furthermore, he used to use perfume immediately after each ritual ablution (*wuḍu'*). When he went out of his house, people noticed his fragrant smell.

Thus, the only way of understanding the Prophetic traditions, as discussed earlier in this paper, is to refer to the Holy Qur'an and other sayings of the Prophet. Using this method, Ibn Arabi tried to find a mystical understanding of this hadith. His discussion concentrated on the central theme of the Prophet's saying; namely love. In Islam and hence, for the Prophet too, love remains a central theme, both when we turn to God and when we want to approach people in society.

Bibliography

1) Fayḍ Kāshāni, Muhammad Ibn Murtada (Mulla Muhsin), *Al-Mahajjah al-Bayḍā'*, Vol. 3. Tehran: Maktabat al-Saduq, 1340 SAH/1961 AD.

2) Gazaali, Abu Haamid Muhammad Ibn Muhammad, *Ihyā' 'Ulum al-Din*, Vol. 4. Cairo: Matba'at al-Uthmāniyyah al-Misriyyah, 1352AH/1933 AD.

3) Hākim al-Nisaabouri, Abu Abd Allah Muhammad, *Al-Mustadrak 'Alā al-Sahihayn fi al-Hadith,* Vol. 2. al-Riyāḍ: Maktabat al-Nasr al-Hadithah, 1968 AD.

4) Huurr al-'Amili, Muhammad Ibn al-Hasan, *Wasā'il al-Shi'ah,* Vol. 7, p. 14. Tehran: al-Maktabah al-Islāmiyyah, 1977 AD.

5) Ibn Arabi, Muhy al-Din, *Fusus al-Hilkam,* Ed. al-'Afifi Abu al-Alā. Beirut: Dār al-Kitāb al-'Arabi, 1949 AD.

6) Ibn Hanbal, Ahmad, *Musnad*, Vol. 3. Beirut: Dār al-Fikr, 1980 AD.

7) Ibn Manzur, *Lisān al-'Arab al-Muhit*, Vol. 5. Beirut: Dār al-Jil, 1408 AH/1988 AD.

8) Khumayni, Ayatollah Sayyid Ruhullah, *Ta'liqāt 'alā Sharh Fusus al-Hikam wa Misbāh al-Uns*, Tehran: Pasdar-i Islam, 1406AH/1986AD.

9) Lane, E. W., *Arabic-English Lexicon*, Vol. 2. London: The Islamic Texts Society, 1984AD.

10) Majlisi, Muhammad, *Bihār al-Anwār al-Jāmi'ah li Durar Akhbār al-A'immah al-Athār,* Vols. 100. Beirut: Mu'assasat al-Wafā, 1983 AD.

11) Muttaqi, 'Alā' al-Din Ali, *Kanz al-Ummāl fi Sunan al-Aqwāl wa al-Af'āl*, Halab: Maktabat al-Turāth al-Islāmi, 1969AD.

12) Nassā'i, Ahmad Ibn Shu'ayb, *Sunan al-Nassā'i*, Commented by al-Suyuti Jalāl al-Din. Vol. 7. Cairo: Maktabat Mustafā Muhammad, 1930 AD.

13) Saduq, Abi Ja'far Muhammad Ibn Ali Bābawayh al-Qummi, *Khisāl*, Vols. 1 & 2. Ed. S. M. M. Al-Sayyid Hasan al-Khurāsān. al-Najaf: al-Matba'ah al-Haydariyyah, 1391 AH/1971 AD.

14) Tabataba'ei, Sayyid Muhammad Husayn, *Sunan al-Nabi*, Ed. and trans. M. H. Fiqhi. Tehran: Kitābfurushi-i Islāmiyyah, 1366 SAH/ 1 987 AD.

15) Tusi, Abi Ja'far Muhammad Ibn al-Hasan, *Amāli*, Vol. 2. Baghdad: al-Maktabat al-Ahliyyah, 1384 AH/1964 AD.

16) ------ *Tahdhib al-Ahkām fi Sharh al-Muqni'ah,* Ed. Musavi, S. H. al-Najaf: Dār al-Kutub al-Islāmiyyah, 1961 AD.

---

[1] The Arabic text is as follows:

"فلما في النّساء من روائح التكوين"

[2] The Arabic text is asfollows:

"فانّ اطيب الطيب عناق الحبيب"

See Ibn Arabi, *Fusus al-Hikam*, p. 220.

[3] For example, the Qur'an says: "But God has endeared the faith to you and has made it seemly in your hearts, and he has made hateful to you unbelief and transgression and disobedience." (49:7)

[4]-See Ahmad Ibn Hanbal, Musnad, Vol. 3, pp. 128 & 285; al-Nassaa'i, *Kitāb al-Sunan*, 'Ishrat al-Nisā, Vol. 7, p. 61; al-Muttaqi, *Kanz al-'Ummāl*, Vol. 6, p.673 cites the hadith as "*min 'aysh al-dunyā*"; Saduq Ibn Babwayh, Al-

Khisāl, Vol. 1, p.154; Majlisi, *Bihār al-Anwār*, Vol. 73, p. 141 & Vol. 100, p. 218.

5 See Ghazali, *Ihyā*, Kitāb al-Mahabbah, p. 255; Fayḍ, *Al-Mahajjah al-Bayḍā*, Vol. 3, p. 68; al-Hurr al-'Amili, *Wasā'il al-Shi'ah*, Vol. 7, p.10 citing from Kulayni, *Furu' al-Kāfi*, Vol. 2, p. 2; Majlisi, *Bihār al-Anwār*, Vol. 73, p. 141; al-Nassa'i, *Kitāb al-Sunan*, 'Ishrat al-Nisā, Vol. 7, p. 61.

[6] Al-Hākim, Kitāb al-Mustadrak, Vol. 2, p.106; Ahmad Ibn Hanbal, Musnad,.Vol. 3, p. 199.

[7] Jalāl al-Din al-Suyuti's comments on *Sunan* of Al-Nassā'i, Vol. 7, p. 62.

[8] It is quoted from Imam Ali (A.S) that once a group of the Prophet's companions abstained from having sexual intercourse with their wives, from sleeping at night and from eating during the day. When Umm al-Salamah (the Prophet's wife) informed the Prophet, he immediately went to them and said: "Do you leave women?! I go toward women. I eat during the day and I sleep at night. He who puts away my tradition, is not from me (my follower)." Based on this narration, the Prophet's behavior can be considered as a perfect role model which prevents_extremism from flourishing. See Tabataba'i, *Sunan al-Nabi*, p. 147.

12 "The love of desires, of women and sons ....is made to seem fair to people; that is the provision of the life of this world..."

13 "O Lord! grant us in our wives and our offspring the joy of our life, and make us guides to pious people."

[11] See Ahmad Ibn Hanbal, *Musnad*, Vol. 3, pp. 128, 199 & 285; *Sunan* of Al-Nassā'i, Vol. 7, pp. 61 & 62; Saduq Ibn Babawayh, *Khisāl*, Vol. 1, p. 154. Interestingly Hākim in his *Mustadrak* quotes the hadith without either *dunyā* or *thalāth*.

[12] Al-Muttaqi, *Kanz al-'Ummāl*, Vol. 6, p. 673:

"ما أحببت من عيش الدنيا إلا الطيب و النّساء"

Al-Hurr al-'Amili, Wasā'il al-Shi'ah, Vol. 7, p. 10 citing from Kulayni, *Furu' al-Kāfii*, Vol. 2, p. 2:

"ما أحببت من دنياكم إلا الطيب و النساء"

[13] Ahmad Ibn Hanbal, Musnad, Vol. 1, pp. 245, 255 & 296:

"إنّ جيرئيل قال للنبىّ (ص): إنّه قد حبّب إليک الصلوة فخذ منها ما شئت"

Tabataba'i also cites another hadith which emphasizes the importance of prayer. See *Sunan al-Nabi*, p. 269. Quotes from Shaykh Tusi, *Al-Amāli*, Vol. 2, p. 141:

" عن النبىّ (ص) قال: يا أباذرّ! إنّ الله تعالى جعل قرّة عينى فى الصلوة و حبّبها إلىّ"

[14]-This is like what is narrated by Kulayni in his *Kitāb al-Kāfi*, Vol. 5, p. 320 and *Furu' al-Kāfi*, Vol. 2, p. 2 as:

"قال رسول الله(ص): جعل قرة عيني في الصلوة و لذتي (في الدنيا) في النساء "

See also Tabataba'i, *Sunan al-Nabi*, p.147.

[15]- Ahmad Ibn Hanbal, *Musnad*, Vol. 3, pp. 128, 199 & 285; Saduq Ibn Babiwayh, *Kitāb al-Khisāl,* Vol. 1, p.154.

[16] E. W. Lane, *Arabic-English Lexicon*, Vol. 2. See also Ibn Manzur, *Lisān al-'Arab*, Vol. 5, pp. 53 & 54.

[17]- Tabaaba'i, *Sunan al-Nabi,* p. 269. Quotes from Shaykh usi, *Al-Amāli*, Vol. 2, p. 141.

[18] "فصّ حكمة فردية في كلمة محمدية"

[19]- Ibn Arabi, *Fusus al-Hikam*, Fass 27, p. 214. One should also note the divine saying (*al-Hadith al-Qudsi*) which says: "I (God) was a hidden treasure then I loved to be known, hence I created". See also Imam Khumayni, *Ta'liqāt 'alā Sharh Fusus al-Hikam wa Misbaah al-Uns*, (Tehran: Paasdar-i Islam, 1406AH/1986AD), p.56. Quotes from *Masābih al-Anwār*, Vol. 2, p.405.

[20]- Ibid, p.216.

[21]- Ibid. See also Ibid, p. 215.

[22] Ibid. p. 220.

[23] "من عرف نفسه فقد عرف ربّه"

[24] Ibid. p. 223: "أنا جليس من ذكرني"

[25]- It is narrated that 'Ayishah (the Prophet's wife) said:

"كان رسول الله (ص) يحدّثنا و نحدّثه فإذا حضرت الصلوة فكأنه لم يعرفنا و لم نعرفه"

> The messenger of God used to talk with us and we used to talk with him, when it was the time of praying then it seemed that he never knew us and we never knew him.

This shows that although the Prophet loved his wives, his deep love was devoted to talking with God. See Tabataba'i, *Sunan al-Nabi,* p. 251 citing from al-Shahid al-Thāni, *Asrār al-Salāt*, pp. 18 & 23 and Majlisi, *Bihār al-Anwār*, Vol. 84, p. 257.

[26] Tabataba'i, *Sunan al-Nabi*, pp. 97 & 98.

Pearls of Wisdom: A Selection of Hadiths from the Prophet Muhammad

Husayn Naghavi

The Prophet Muhammad (pbuh) has spoken about various aspects of human life, both worldly and heavenly, and his words are curative prescriptions for the various problems of human beings. In addition to the sayings quoted in this paper, he has many others on topics too numerous to mention, and as diverse as women, children, orphans, justice, government, leisure and sport, entertainment, selflessness and sympathy, self-restraint, truthfulness, watchfulness, cheating, oppression, relatives, animals and the environment.

I. God and Man

1. "God's kindness towards His creatures is more than a mother's towards her baby."[1]
2. "Remembrance of God is like polish for the heart."[2]
3. "Serve God as you would if you could see Him because although you cannot see Him, He can see you."[3]
4. "God does not look at your appearance or your possessions, but He looks at your heart and your deeds."[4]

II. The Faithful

5. A man asked: "O Prophet of God! What is faith?" The Prophet said: "You are a person of faith when your good deed gives you pleasure and your evil deed grieves you."[5]

6. "A believer is like a mirror to another believer. A believer is a brother to another believer." [6]

7. "The most faithful of you are the best mannered." [7]

8. "Believers are like the different parts of a building, each one supporting the other." [8]

9. "You will observe that the believers are like parts of the body in relation to each other in matters of kindness, love and affection. When one part of the body is afflicted, the entire body feels it, there is loss of sleep and a fever develops." [9]

III. The True Muslim

10. "The perfect Muslim is not perfect if he eats until he is full and yet leaves his neighbours hungry." [10]

11. "A perfect Muslim is the one from whose tongue and hands his fellow brothers and sisters are safe." [11]

IV. Wisdom, Knowledge and Thought

12. "Fearing God is the peak (or source) of wisdom." [12]

13. "Ignorance is the worst kind of poverty, intellectuality is the greatest of riches, and thought is the best form of worship." [13]

14. "Seek knowledge even in China because acquiring knowledge is obligatory for every Muslim." [14]

15. "Seek knowledge from the cradle to the grave." [15]

16. "Retain knowledge by writing it down (recording it)." [16]

V. Society

17. "The best people are those who are the most useful to others." [17]

18. "A moment of justice is better than a year of worship." [18]

19. "Cursed be he who imposes his burden on people." [19]

20. "The best struggle (*jihad*) is a just word before a tyrannical authority."[20]

VI. Friendship and Love

21. "It is better to sit alone than in the company of bad people and it is even better to sit with good people rather than alone. It is better to speak to a seeker of knowledge than to remain silent; but silence is better than idle words."[21]

22. The Prophet of Islam said: "The Apostles said to Jesus: "O Spirit of Allah! With whom should we keep company?" He said: "The person the sight of whom reminds you of God, the speech of whom increases your knowledge and the deeds of whom make you desirous of the other world."""[22]

23. "Seven people shall be sheltered by God in the Shade of His Throne when there will be no shade except His Shade… and two people that love each other for the sake of God…."[23]

VII. Family Ties

24. "The best person among you is the one who treats his family members the best and I am the person who treats his family in the best way."[24]

25. A man once told the Prophet that he had many children but had not kissed any of them. The Prophet (pbuh) replied: "Verily, God will only show mercy to those of His servants who show mercy to others."[25]

26. A person came to the Messenger of God (pbuh) and asked, "Who among people is most deserving of my good treatment?"' He said, "Your mother, then your mother, then your mother, then your father, then those closest to you, then those closest to you"[26]

27. "A child's affectionate look at their parents is a form of worship."[27]

28. "Paradise is under the feet of mothers."[28]

VIII. Equality of Human Beings

29. "The God of all people is the same and the father of all people is the same. All of you are children of Adam and Adam was made from earth. The most honorable of you in God's estimation is the most pious."[29]

30. "Be careful because you are not better than people who are a different color, unless you are better in piety."[30]

IX. Neighbours

31. "Gabriel (the Angel of Revelation) is always instructing me about neighbours, so much so that I think that neighbours may inherit from their neighbours."[31]

32. "The person whose neighbour is not safe from his bad behaviour will not enter Heaven."[32]

X. Peace

33. "Forgive him who wrongs you, re-unite with him who cuts you off, do good to him who does you harm and speak the truth although it may be to your disadvantage."[33]

34. "Do you know what is better than charity, fasting, and prayer? It is keeping peace and good relations between people, as quarrels and bad feelings destroy mankind." 34

XI. Good Conduct and Morality

35. "If you guarantee me six things on your part, I shall guarantee you Paradise: Speak the truth when you talk, keep a promise when you make it, when you are trusted with something fulfill your trust, avoid sexual immorality, lower your gaze (out of modesty) and prevent your hands and tongue from committing injustice."[35]

36. "The best people are the best mannered."[36 & 37]

37. "On the Day of Resurrection nothing will weigh heavier in the scale of the believer than good manners."[38]

38. "When you see flatterers, throw dust in their faces."[39]

39. "Whoever is kind, God will be kind to him; therefore be kind to man on earth. He Who is in heaven will then show mercy to you."[40]

40. "If Prophet Muhammad (pbuh) heard the crying of a child in the company of its mother during prayer, he would recite only a short chapter of the Holy Qur'an (in order to finish the prayer more quickly and let the mother comfort her child)."[41]

41. "Love of this world is the origin of every sin."[42]

XII. Control of Anger

42. "Anger is like the devil. The devil has been created from fire and fire is extinguished by water. Therefore, when any of you feels angry, you should perform ablution".[43]

43. "Three things are part of the good morals of a believer. When he is overcome by anger, his anger should not drive him to falsehood. When he is happy, his happiness should not take him beyond the bounds of what is right. When he has power, he should not stake a claim to something which is not his."[44]

XIII. Modesty

44. "Modesty (hayaa) does not bring anything except good."[45]

45. "God has revealed to me that you must be humble. No one should boast over another, and no one should oppress another."[46]

46. "If you do not feel ashamed of anything, then you may do whatever you like."[47]

XIV. Patience

47. "How wonderful is the situation of a believer. There is good for him in everything and this applies only to a believer. If prosperity comes to him, he expresses gratitude to God and that is good for him; and if adversity befalls him, he endures it patiently and that is better for

him."[48]

48. "Understand that victory comes to the one who is patient."[49]

XV. The Golden Rule

49. "None of you (truly) believes until he wishes for his brother what he wishes for himself."[50]

XVI. Harmfulness of Envy

50. "Truly, envy eats up and takes away good deeds as fire eats up and burns wood."[51]

Bibliography

- 'Amili, Sayyed Muhammad b. Muhammad b. Hasan, *Ithna 'Ashariyya fi al-Mawaa'iz al-'Adadiyya*, (Qum: Hekmah Publication, without date.)
- Harrani, Abu Muhammed al-Hasan b. Ali (2001), *Tuhaf al-'Uqul,* Trans. by Badr Shahin, (Qum: Ansariyan Publications)
- Kulayni, Muhammad (1379 A.H), *Al-Furu' Min al-Kafi*, (Tehran: Dar al-Kutub al-Islamiyah)
- Kulayni, Muhammad (1388 A.H), *Usul al-Kafi* (Tehran: Dar al-Kutub al-Islamiyah)
- Majlisi, Muhammad Baqir (1983), *Bihar al-Anwar* (Beirut: Al-Wafa)
- Nishaburi, Muhammad b. al-Fattal (1386), *Rawdat al-Waa'izin*,(Qum: al-Sharif al-Razi Publications)
- Payande, Abulqasim (1337), *Nahj al-Fasaha*, (Tehran: al-Islamiyya Publication)
- Waseti, Ali b. Muhammad al-Laysi (1376), *'Uyun al-Hikam wa al-Mawaa'iz*, (Qum: Dar al-Hadis)

---

[1] إن الله تعالي أرحم بعبده من الوالده المشفقه بولدها. (*Rawdat al-Waaezin*, p. 503)

[2] ذكر الله جلاء الصدور ...(*'Uyun al-Hikam wa al-Mawaa'iz*, p. 256)

[3] أعبدِالله كأنك تراه فإن كنتَ لاتراه فإنّه يراكَ. (*Nahj al-Fasaha*, No 335)

[4] إنّ الله تعالي لاينظر الي صوركم و اموالكم ولكن ينظر الي قلوبكم و اعمالكم.(Ibid. No. 719.)
[5] إذا سرّتك حسنتك و ساءتك سيئتك فأنت مؤمن.

(Ibid. No 215 and *Ithna 'Ashariyya fi al-Mawaa'iz al-'Adadiyya*, p. 10)

[6] المؤمن مرآت المؤمن، المؤمن أخ المؤمن.

(Ithna 'Ashariyya fi al-Mawaa'iz al-'Adadiyya, p. 8)

[7] افضلكم ايماناً احسنكم اخلاقاً

(Nahj al-Fasaha, No. 420 and *Tuhaf al-'Uqul*, No. 69.)

[8] ألمؤمن للمؤمن كالبناء يشتد بعضه بعضاً

(Ithna 'Ashariyya fi al-Mawaa'iz al-'Adadiyya, p. 8)

[9] مثل المؤمنين في توادّهم و تراحمهم كمثل الجسد أذا اشتكي بعضهم تداعي سائرهم بالسهر و الحمي. (*Nahj al-Fasaha*, No. 2712.)

This tradition is narrated from Imam Sadiq like this:

المؤمن أخو ألمؤمن كالجسد الواحد، أن اشتكي شيئا منه وجد ألم ذلک في سائر جسده ...

(*Usül al-Kafi*, Vol. 2, p. 133)

[10] ما أمن بالله و اليوم الاخر من بات شبعان و جاره جائع

(*Bihar al-Anwar,* Vol. 75, p. 273)

[11] المسلم من سلم المسلمون من يده و لسانه

(Ithna 'Ashariyya fi al-Mawaa'iz al-'Adadiyya, p. 8)

[12] رأس الحكمة مخافة الله (Ibid.)

[13] لافقر أشدّ من الجهل و لا مال أعود من العقل ... و لاعباده مثل التفكّر.

(Nahj al-Fasaha, No. 2505)

[14] أطلبوا العلم و لو بالصين فإنّ طلب العلم فريضه علي كلّ مسلم.(Ibid. No. 324.)

[15] أطلبوا العلم من المهد الي اللحد. (Ibid. No. 327.)

[16] قيّدوا العلم بالكتاب. (Tuhaf al-'Uqul, No. 8 and Ithna 'Ashariyya, p. 14)

[17] سئل رسول الله صل الله عليه و آله من آحب الناس ألي الله؟ قال: أنفع الناس للناس.

(Usül al-Kafi, Vol. 2, p. 131)

[18] عدل ساعة خيرٌ من عبادة سنة. (*Nahj al-Fasaha*, No. 1936)

[19] ملعون من القي كَلّه علي الناس. (*Tuhaf al-'Uqul*, No. 19)

[20] أفضل الجهاد كلمه حقّ عند سلطانٍ جائر. (*Nahj al-Fasaha*, No. 394)

[21] الوحدة خيرٌ من جليس السوء و الجليس الصالح خيرٌ من الوحدة و أملاء الخير خيرٌ من السكوت و السكوت خيرٌ من أملاء الشر. (*Nahj al-Fasaha*, No. 3194)

[22] .. قالوا: يا روح الله فمن نجالس أذاً؟ قال: من يذكّركم الله رؤيته و يزيد في عملكم منطقه و يرغّبكم في الاخره عمله. (*Tuhaf al-'Uqul*, No. 60.)

[23] سبعة يظلهم الله تحت ظل عرشه يوم لاظل ألا ظله: ... و رجلان تحابا في الله ...

(Nahj al-Fasaha, No. 1731 & 1732.)

The Prophet also said: "If a man loves his brother in faith, he should tell him that he loves him." (Ibid. No. 1520)

[24] خيركم خيركم لأهله و أنا خيركم لأهلي (Ibid. No. 1520)

[25] أن رسول الله كان يقبل الحسن بن علي عليهما السلام فقال الاقرع بن حابس: أن لي عشرة من الولد ما قبلت أحداً منهم فقال رسول الله (ص): من لا يرحم لا يرحم.

(*Rawdat al-Waaezin*, p. 369)

[26] امّک أمّک ثمّ أمّک ثمّ أباک ثمّ الاقرب فالاقرب. (*Nahj al-Fasaha*, No. 546.)

[27] نظر الولد الي والديه حبّاً لهما عباده. (*Tuhaf al-'Uqul*, No. 79.)

[28] الجنة تحت اقدام الامّهات (*Ithna 'Ashariyya fi al-Mawaa'iz al-'Adadiyya*, p. 8)

[29] أيها الناس إنّ ربّكم واحدٌ و أنّ أباكم واحدٌ، كلّكم لآدم و آدم من ترابٍ إنّ أكرمكم عندالله اتقاكم. (*Nahj al-Fasaha*, No. 1044)

[30] أنظر فإنّک لست بخيرٍ من احمر و لا أسود ألّا أن تفضله بتقوي. (Ibid. No. 562)

[31] ما زال جبريل يوصينيّ بالجار حتي ظننت أنه سيورثه. (Ibid. No. 2640)

[32] لايدخل الجنة عبدٌ لايأمن جاره بواغيه (*Ithna 'Ashariyya*, p15)

[33] واعف عمّن ظلمک و صل من قطعک و أحسن إلي من أساء اليک وقل الحق و لو علي نفسک. (*Nahj al-Fasaha*, No. 1842 and *Usul al-Kafi*, Vol. 2, p. 87)

[34] ألا أخبركم بأفضل من درجة الصيام و الصلوة و الصدقة؟ صلاح ذات البين فإنّ فساد ذات البين هي الحالقة. (*Nahj al-Fasaha*, No. 458.)

[35] تقبلوا اليّ بستٍ أتقبل لكم بالجنّة إذا تحدّثتم فلاتكذّبوا و أذا وعدتم فلاتخلفوا و أذا ائتمنتم فلاتخونوا و غضّوا ابصاركم و احفظوا فروجكم و كفّوا أيديكم و ألسنتكم (*Ithna 'Ashariyya*, p. 226)

[36] See also No 7.

[37] خيرٌ الناس أحسنهم خُلقاً. (*Nahj al-Fasaha*, No. 1498)

[38] ليس شيءٌ أثقل في الميزان من الخُلق الحسن. (Ibid, No. 2397)

[39] أحثوا الترابَ في وجوه المدّاحين. (Ibid. No. 91)

[40] الرّاحمون يرحمهم الرحمن تبارک و تعالي إرحموا مَن في الارض يرحمكم مَن في السماء. (Ibid. No. 1679 and *Ithna 'Ashariyya*, p. 14)

[41] صلّي رسول الله (ص) بالناس الظهر فخفّف في الركعتين الاخيرتين. فلمّا انصرف قال له الناس: هل حدث في الصلاه حدث؟ ... فقال لهم: أما سمعتم صراخ الصبي؟ (Al-Furu' Min al-Kafi, Vol. 6, p. 48)

[42] حب الدّنيا رأس كل خطيئة (*Nahj al-Fasaha*, No. 1342)

[43] أنّ الغضب من الشيطان و أنّ الشيطان خُلق من النار و إنّما تُطفأ النار بالماء فإذا غضِبَ أحدكم فليتوضّأ. (Ibid. No. 660)

[44] ثلاثٌ من اخلاق الايمان: مَن إذا غضِب لم يدخله غضبه في الباطل و مَن إذا رَضي لم يخرجه رضاه مِن الحقّ و مَن إذا قَدَر لم يتعاط ما ليس له. (Ibid. No. 1267)

[45] الحياء لا يأتي إلا بخير. (Ibid. No. 1426 and *Ithna 'Ashariyya*, p. 8)

[46] إنّ الله أوحي الي أن تواضعوا حتّي لايفخر أحدٌ علي أحد و لا يبغي أحد علي أحدٍ. (*Nahj al-Fasaha*, No. 678)

[47] إذا لم تستحيي فاصنع ما شئتَ. (Ibid. No. 238)

[48] عجباً لأمر المؤمن, إنّ أمره كلّه خيرٌ و ليس ذلک لأحدٍ إلا للمؤمن إن أصابته سرّاء شكر و كان خيراً له و إن اصابته ضرّاء صبر و كان خيراً له. (Ibid. No. 1932)

[49] إعلم أنّ النصر مع الصبر... (Ibid. No. 363)

[50] لايؤمن عبدٌ حتّي يحب لأخيه مايحب لنفسه من الخير (*Ithna 'Ashariyya*, p. 15)

[51] أنّ الحسد ليأكل الحسنات كما تأكل النار الحطب. (Ibid. p. 17)